LANCASHIRE COUNTY LIBRARY

This book must be returned on or before the date marked below

TOO CLEVER FOR LOVE

A Comedy in Three Acts

by

WALTER GREENWOOD

LONDON

SAMUEL FRENCH LIMITED

SAMUEL FRENCH LTD
26 SOUTHAMPTON STREET, STRAND, LONDON, W.C.2

SAMUEL FRENCH INC.
25 WEST 45TH STREET, NEW YORK, U.S.A.
7623 SUNSET BOULEVARD, HOLLYWOOD 46, CAL.

SAMUEL FRENCH (CANADA) LTD
27 GRENVILLE STREET, TORONTO

SAMUEL FRENCH (AUSTRALIA) PTY LTD
159 FORBES STREET, SYDNEY

MADE AND PRINTED IN GREAT BRITAIN BY
RICHARD   WHEWELL   (BOLTON),   LTD.,
FOLDS ROAD, BOLTON.

TOO CLEVER FOR LOVE

First produced by Douglas Emery at the Oldham Repertory Theatre under the title *Never a Dull Moment*. The present version, under its new title, was produced by Mervyn R. Pinfield at the Morecambe Repertory Theatre.

CHARACTERS

(*in the order of their appearance*)

JAMES BLAIR

JOAN BLAIR, his sister

MR BLAIR (Pa), their father

MRS BLAIR (Ma), their mother

MRS DORBELL, a neighbour

HELEN BLAIR, Joan's sister

RICHARD SANDERS

SAM BALCOMBE

BETTY SANDERS, Richard's sister

TOM HOLROYD, landlord of the *Rose and Crown*

SYNOPSIS OF SCENES

ACT I

The Blairs' Living-room. Evening

ACT II

Scene 1 The same. Evening, a few days later

Scene 2 The "Best Room" of the *Rose and Crown*. Next Evening

ACT III

The Blairs' Living-room. Evening, some time later

TOO CLEVER FOR LOVE

———

ACT I

SCENE.—*The Blairs' living-room. Evening.*

The Blairs' home is a respectable one which might be found in any north country industrial town, or, it if comes to that, in any other part of Britain. MR BLAIR *is working, as are the three grown up children,* JAMES, JOAN *and* HELEN, *so that the combined income makes the family comfortably off. The walls of the living-room are wall-papered with a bold pattern. The front door, which opens directly into the room, is* C. *of the back wall. A window* R. *of the door overlooks the street. Up* R., *there is a staircase, of which the two bottom steps can be seen, with a door to close it off from the room. A door down* R. *leads to the kitchen, scullery and back yard. The fireplace, of the kitchen-range type, is* L. *There are comfortable armchairs above and below the fireplace. A chest of drawers stands* L. *of the door up* C. *There is an oval table in the window bay, an occasional table down* L. *and a small table below the door down* R. *with a radio receiver on it. The sideboard stands above the door down* R. *There is a dining-table* R.C. *with dining-chairs* R., L. *and above it. A fourth dining-chair stands* R. *of the table in the window. The room is carpeted and there are net and draw-curtains at the window. An assortment of pictures decorate the walls. At night the room is lit by a shaded electric pendant hanging* C. *Sundry coats and other garments hang from hooks behind the front door.*

(*See the Ground Plan and Photograph of the Scene.*)

When the CURTAIN *rises, the fire is lit, the doors are closed, but the window curtains are open.* MR BLAIR (PA) *is seated in the armchair above the fireplace, reading a newspaper.* JAMES *is seated* R. *of the table, studying a newspaper. His football pools coupon and a pencil are on the table in front of him. He is in his late twenties.* JOAN, *the youngest of the family, is seated in the armchair below the fire-place. She is lolling in the chair, and her left leg is hooked over the arm of it. Her hair is in paper curlers. She is reading a novelette. She is tomboyish, inclined to plumpness, and has the good nature usually associated with it.* MRS BLAIR (MA) *enters down* R. *She carries an empty tray. She still has remnants of her youthful beauty. She wears a clean starched apron with a bib over her*

1

frock. She is soft-hearted, a failing of which her less scrupulous neighbours are always ready to take advantage. She puts the tray on the table and begins to gather up the tea things.

JAMES (*without looking up*). Don't empty the teapot, Ma.

MA. This'll be stone cold—and I'm brewing no more. Ration won't run it.

JAMES. What's in the pot'll do for me.

MA. I'll have you know I've not got all night to be muckin' about. Mrs Dorbell'll be here in a minute. (*She pours a cup of tea for* JAMES.)

JAMES. What's bringing her round ?

MA. Food parcels have arrived from Australia. I'm going round with her for company and pick up your grandma's parcel at the same time.

JAMES. Trust Ma Dorbell to be around when there's something for nothing going.

MA. Leave the old girl alone, our James. If you've worked as hard as she's done when you're her age, you'll not have done so badly.

(*The front door up* L.C. *opens.* MRS DORBELL *enters and announces herself. She is an old crone. Usually she wears a shawl but now she has on a tight fitting, moth-eaten coat whose shabby fur collar cannot now be identified with that of any animal. She also wears a battered hat with a broken feather in it. She limps painfully as she walks.*)

MRS DORBELL. I'm comin' in. Ooo, me feet, me feet. Let me get sat down. Thought I'd get dressed up. Had to redeem me best shoes. Twelve months since I had 'em out last for Mrs Mac's funeral. Let me get sat down. Let me get sat down. These shoes're going back up the spout first thing next morning. Give me me old slippers any time. (*She sits* L. *of the table and reaches to caress her feet.*) Ooo. How I'm going to get there *and* back I don't know.

MA (*passing the cup of tea to* JAMES). There you are, our James.

(JAMES *reaches for the sugar which* MRS BLAIR *whips from under his hand.*)

JAMES. Eh, Ma—only a spoonful.

MA. You're getting none for slop like that.

(JAMES *tries unsuccessfully to snatch the sugar basin and accidentally knocks some of the tea on to his football coupons.*)

JAMES. There. Now see what you've done. All over my blooming coupons.

MA. Never mind your coupons. Get the tea supped and let me get cleared up and done with.

MRS DORBELL. 'Bout time they were married and homes of their own if you ask me. They'd have more to do with their time than jazzin' and football poolin'.

JAMES. Married ? Me ? That'll be the day.

MA. You'll come to it, don't fret.

JAMES. Maybe. But it'll be when you can sack a wife like you can a housekeeper. Not before. I've been around, you know.

JOAN. We know. Acting lance corporal—unpaid.

JAMES. I was there, anyway, and that's more than can be said of some of those stand back fusiliers you muck around with on the dance floor.

MA. Do you want this tea or don't you ?

JAMES. Course I do. Won the war, this did.

MRS DORBELL. Well, wi' things as they are I can't see we'd have been much worse off if we'd lost it.

JAMES. I don't know what we'd have done without the old cuppa char in the army.

MA. You'd have had to do the same as us at home. Do without. We were rationed, you know.

MRS DORBELL. Still are. An' Labour in for five years.

JAMES. Give 'em a chance, Mrs Dorbell.

JOAN. We did. And the first thing they did was to vote 'emselves an extra four hundred a year raise.

MRS DORBELL. Don't forget the perks. Don't forget the perks. Her in the next street whose husband got elected is swankin' about with a fur coat on now. An' *both* their lads soon got a nice cushy job on the Coal Board when he went into Parlyment.

JAMES. Give 'em a chance, that's what I say. And don't forget it, Mrs Dorbell. They raised your old age pension.

MRS DORBELL. I'd rather have the ten bob I got before the war. You *could* buy something with it. I'll be damned if you can now.

JOAN. *I've* got a vote next time. And I'll tell you this. Labour won't get it. Millions of nylons we're making at the factory. None for us—all for export.

JAMES. Unconscious. Politically unconscious, all of you. (*He shouts.*) They've done the best they could.

JOAN. Who for ?

JAMES. Oh, you give me the willies. All of you. The blooming willies.

(MR BLAIR *rises and, with newspaper in hand, crosses without a word to the door* R.)

MA. Where're you off to, Father ?

PA. Down the backyard. The only place where a feller can get a bit of peace and quiet in this house.

(*He exits* R.)

MA. There. See. He's been set off now. That's all your fault, our James. You and your politics.

JAMES. Me ? Sitting here quiet, minding my own business and doing no harm to nobody. Trying to do my coupons.

MRS DORBELL. Coupons for meat, coupons for grocery, coupons for blooming toffee and you muck about wi' more for pleasure.

JOAN. He might win a fortune. Ha, ha, ha.

MA. Your father's been trying that for years and where is he now ?

MRS DORBELL. Down the backyard.

(JOAN *rises and crosses to the staircase up* R.)

JOAN. And I'm going to get ready. (*To* JAMES.) And listen, you. I've a young man coming. If he gets here before I come down please to mind your own business. And if Sam Balcombe comes round with my nylons they're paid for, and tell him Annie Marsh wants a pair of black. (*She goes off muttering.*) Making them and having to buy them on the black-market.

(*She exits up the stairs.*)

JAMES. He'll get pinched one of these days, will that Sam Balcombe. Talk about a never-work.

MRS DORBELL. There's none of you young 'uns any room to talk of never workin'. Five days a week, eh ? No wonder there's no unemployment. No wonder we're havin' to bring in foreigners. Puh ! When I was . . .

JAMES. I know. Four looms. Six of a morning till six at night. Those days're done with. *We've* seen to that.

MRS DORBELL. Not the only thing that's done with. A square meal's been done away with, too. What's more—it's started agen.

JAMES. What has ?

MRS DORBELL. Queuein' up at pawnshop.

(*While* MRS DORBELL *is speaking* MRS BLAIR *suddenly claps her hand to her mouth.*)

MA. My God !

JAMES. Now what's up, Ma ?

MA. My purse ! It's gone !

JAMES. Aw ! Not again, Ma. Four times a day it disappears. Look in your pocket. That's where it usually is.

MA. You mind your own business, Mr Clever Devil. I had it in my hands when I was getting the rations.

MRS DORBELL. I never bother if I lose mine. There's never anything in it.

MA. Oh, my God ! And the ration books, too. See whether they're on the shelf, our James.

(JAMES, *muttering, rises, crosses to the fireplace and looks on the mantelpiece.*)

JAMES. Blooming purse and blooming ration books.

(MRS BLAIR *crosses hurriedly to the chest of drawers and rummages in one of them in which she keeps her things.*)

Mrs Dorbell.   Government only keeps rationin' on to give soft jobs to their pals.

Ma.   They aren't here.

James.   Not here, either.   I wish you'd be more careful.

Ma.   I *am* careful.   It's all this rationin' an' queuein' business. It gets me all flustered.   Oh, what am I going to do ?

James.   Try your coat, like I say.

Ma.   Stop mitherin' me.   I know they're not there.   (*She turns, in a panic, to the front door behind which her coat is hanging.   She feels in the pocket and finds the books.*)   Thank God !   But my purse is gone.   I knew it.   I knew it.

James.   Feel in your skirt pocket.

Ma.   Oh, will you stop tellin' me what to do.

Mrs Dorbell.   Do as the lad says, love.

Ma (*absently feeling in her skirt pocket*).   I know where I left it. Shop counter.   It'll have gone.   (*She finds purse.*)   Oh, it's here.

James.   Told you.

Ma.   Could have sworn I left it on the counter.   (*She removes her apron, hangs it behind the front door, picks up her hat from the chest of drawers, and puts it on.*)

Mrs Dorbell.   Nobody ever leaves a purse on the counter when I'm in a shop.   It's last they'd ever see of it if I got my hands on it.

Ma.   When our Helen comes in tell her her tea's in the oven. Like to know what's keeping her at this time of the night.   Now, where's my coat ?   Ready in a minute, Mrs Dorbell.   Sorry to keep you waitin'.   (*She takes her coat from the hook behind the front door.*)

Mrs Dorbell.   Don't you worry about me.   Only too glad to be sitting down wi' these shoes on.   So long as I'm back before the *Rose and Crown* closes I'll be all right.   That's if I can raise the price of a pint.

James.   You probably will.

Ma.   You mind you don't take a drink too many, Mrs Dorbell. (*She puts on her coat.*)

Mrs Dorbell.   Impossible.   Nearly *was* converted once, though. One o' them chapel going fellers with a bible always in his pocket. Frightened me to death with all the things I was going to die of through drinkin'.   Used to froth at the mouth he did when he held his meetings tellin' everybody how sinful they was.   Then what did he do but drop down dead at a meetin' just after he'd had a sup of water.   That cured *me* o' wantin' to be cured.   Forty he was an' here I am turned seventy and never ailed a day in my life except when I can't get a drink.   Melancholy mad I am without it. Melancholy mad.

Ma.   Our Helen's tea'll be spoiled if she isn't back soon.

Mrs Dorbell.   Don't you worry about her.   She won't be home yet a while.

Ma.   Have you seen her ?

MRS DORBELL. Couldn't miss seeing her. Been on the street corner for the last half hour havin' a row.

MA. Who with?

MRS DORBELL. That young man of hers. Oh, don't worry. The row'll go on for hours. One of those silent ones. They've been standing there for fifteen minutes just starin' at the floor sayin' nowt. Thank God I'm past all that.

MA (*sighing*). Ay, I wish she'd get wed.

MRS DORBELL. Puh! I wouldn't wish that on my worst enemy.

JAMES. I would—if I didn't like him enough.

MRS DORBELL. I've heard your kind talk before. I'd like to lay a bet you're the first married out of this house.

JAMES (*laughing*). What odds are you layin'?

MRS DORBELL. Nay, you lay the odds bein' as you're so confident.

JAMES. You can have ten pounds to a shirt button.

MRS DORBELL. And I'll take it. You hear what he said, Mrs Blair?

MA. I heard. And I only wish he'd do it.

JAMES. Well, Government's giving us every encouragement. Payin' us to have kids.

MRS DORBELL. We had to do it for love. (*She rises.*) Well, come on, Mrs Blair. Let's get those parcels and let me get these shoes off before the pub closes. I deserve the price of a drink for all the agony I've had to put up with wearin' 'em. (*She makes her way painfully to the front door, ooing and ahing at each step.*)

MA. Don't forget what I said about our Helen's tea, our James. (*She talks aloud to herself as she follows* MRS DORBELL *out.*) Children, children, children. The worry of it all.

(MRS DORBELL *and* MRS BLAIR *exit by the front door.* JAMES *lights a cigarette, sighs contentedly, crosses to* R. *of the table and resettles himself comfortably to the study of his coupons.*)

JAMES. Now, let's see. Arsenal—er—win. United a cert. City—mmm. Give 'em one more chance and trŷ 'em with a draw this week. Rovers—now—where's the blooming paper. (*He glances around.*) Oh, aye. He's down the back. (*He rises, crosses to the door* R., *opens it and shouts off.*) You can come out now, Dad. Bring paper with you. (*He resumes his seat at the table.*)

(MR BLAIR *enters* R.)

PA. Have they gone?

JAMES. Aye. But our Joan's upstairs. Expectin' a feller. *Another* new 'un.

PA. Where's our Helen?

JAMES. On the street corner—havin' a row.

PA (*crossing and sitting in the armchair above the fireplace*). Lookin' forward to tonight I was, I wish you'd all take your rows down to the street corner.

JAMES. Why, what've you got on ?

PA. If you want to know I was going to wash my feet. Nearly crippled, I am, with my corns.

JAMES. Well, then, wash 'em.

PA. What, with our Joan upstairs expectin' a young feller. And our Helen comin' in at any moment. You know what she's like. There's enough rows in this house without me bein' the cause of more.

JAMES. If I wanted to soak my poor old feet I'd . . .

PA. We know. You'd soak 'em.

JAMES. I would an' all. No woman'd boss me around. If you ask me the world's never been the same since they gave votes to women.

PA. Your Ma's a woman and I wouldn't like her job running a house now, or during the war.

JAMES. I'm not talking about Ma. I'm talking about the modern young women.

PA. Thought you had nothing to do with young women.

JAMES. I don't.

PA. Then how is it you know so much about them ?

JAMES. I've got eyes, haven't I ? I've got ears, haven't I ? I work with married men, don't I ? Love, eh ? I'm sticking to freedom.

PA. You've got it all worked out.

(HELEN *enters by the front door. She is a handsome girl who takes pride in her appearance. Occasionally,* JAMES *and* JOAN *put this down to swank. That she has had a row with her young man is evident from her expression.* PA *glances at her, then, without a word, rises, crosses to the door* R. *and exits.*)

JAMES. Hullo, misery. What's eating you ?

HELEN (*fiercely*). You leave me alone.

JAMES. All right. All right. Your tea's in the oven.

HELEN. Don't want any.

JAMES. You can go on hunger strike if you like but it's in the oven all the same.

(HELEN *removes her coat, hangs it on a coat-hanger behind the front door, then flops into the armchair above the fireplace, sighs heavily and stares into the flames.*)

Been havin' a row, love ?

(HELEN *ignores the question.*)

HELEN (*after a pause*). Are you going out ?

JAMES. You don't think I'm staying in here when she's having a feller round.

HELEN. Our Joan ?

JAMES. Aye.

HELEN. Where is she?

JAMES (*jerking his thumb at the ceiling*). Getting tarted up. (*He chuckles.*) Bet she isn't half having a go at your things.

(HELEN *leaps up and rushes to the staircase door.*)

HELEN (*calling*). Our Joan.

JOAN (*off*). What?

HELEN. You leave me things alone.

JOAN (*off*). Not touching your mouldy things.

HELEN. You're not going out of here until I see what you've got on. (*She crosses and resumes her seat.*)

JAMES. What's the row about *this* time?

HELEN. Mind your own business.

JAMES. Won't he wed you?

HELEN (*balefully*). One of these days I hope you get it—right in the neck.

JAMES. I'll be drunk or daft or both if I do. I've lived too long with you and our Joan.

(*The sound is heard of a motor bicycle approaching and coming to a stop outside. There is a knock on the front door. HELEN sighs. JAMES rises, crosses to the door, opens it, and returns to the table with an air of weary indifference. He does not look to see who the visitor is.*)

Come in and make yourself at home. They all do.

(RICHARD SANDERS, *a young man, takes a half-hearted step into the room. He is dressed in all the paraphernalia of a motor cyclist. He is a good looking, ingenuous young fellow and obviously is shy.*)

RICHARD. I've—er . . .

JAMES. She's upstairs getting ready. I'd take a load off your feet if I were you.

RICHARD (*sitting* L. *of the table*). Thank you.

JAMES. Once either of 'em get stuck in front of a mirror you never know when they'll finish.

(RICHARD *smiles.*)

What's your name?

RICHARD. Richard Sanders.

JAMES. Workin' or spivvin'?

RICHARD. Ay, I wouldn't be clever enough to be a spiv. I'm electrical engineerin'.

JAMES. That your bike outside?

RICHARD. Aye.

JAMES. New?

RICHARD. Aye. Brough Superior.

JAMES. Paid for?

RICHARD. Oh, aye. Fitted up my old bike when I got demobbed and flogged it. (*He looks at* HELEN.) I mean—I sold it for a good price. So—you know—the new one didn't cost me all that much.

JAMES. Where're you going tonight ?

HELEN. I'd like to apologize for my brother, Mr Sanders. One thing he can't do is to mind his own business. I'm Helen Blair.

(RICHARD *half rises and makes a little bow.*)

RICHARD. How do you do ? I—er . . .

HELEN. Yes ?

RICHARD (*smiling and shrugging*). I thought you might be— you were—his young lady. You don't much look like Joan, you know.

JAMES. That's what she's always hoped. Keep it up, Dick. You're doing fine.

HELEN. There's nothing we can do about my brother's manners. I'm sorry. (*She rises and crosses to the staircase door.*)

JAMES. Hark at her. You should have heard her having a go at me before you came in.

HELEN (*calling through the door*). Joan. Mr Sanders is here.

JOAN (*off*). Down in a minute.

(HELEN *crosses and resumes her seat.*)

HELEN. She's coming.

RICHARD. Thank you.

(HELEN *glances down her nose at* JAMES.)

JAMES. Consider yourself sat on, James. (*To* HELEN.) But wait until you want to borrow any dough from me again, lady. Wait, that's all. (*To* RICHARD.) As for you, lad, if you knew as much about her upstairs as I do you'd be on that bike of yours top gearing it out of here before she comes down.

HELEN. Perhaps so—if he was you. But he doesn't happen to be you so . . .

JAMES. She'd say "put a sock in it" if you weren't here. That's the kind of talk they come out with *after* you've wed 'em.

RICHARD. H'm—er . . .

JAMES. What ?

RICHARD. Do you think she'll be long ?

JAMES. I dunno. You're doing the waiting. Ha ! Think *I'd* wait for a dame ? I'd say "I'll be on the street corner at six o'clock". And if she wasn't there—d'you know what I'd do ?

HELEN. Of course we do. You'd do the girl a good turn and clear off.

JAMES (*ignoring* HELEN). I'll do you a good turn if you like.

RICHARD. Oh ?

JAMES. Aye. I'm training a bird.

RICHARD. Did you say "a bird" ?

JAMES. Aye. But one with feathers on. Pigeon Derby. He's a beaut. Fourteen stray hens he's brought home up to now. He's got something, that bird.

HELEN. That's more than can be said of its owner.

JAMES. Now, if you'd listen to me you'd take me and that bird on your pillion and drive us out to the country so's I could give him a bit of training.

RICHARD. Yes—er—some other time, perhaps. But I couldn't, you know. I've promised to take Joan.

JAMES. Please yourself. But you'll be driving with a heap of trouble sitting right behind you.

HELEN. The heap of trouble's sitting right in front of you, Mr Sanders. He's got too much of what the cat licks itself with.

JAMES. Nice ladylike expressions, aren't they ? Coming from the leading lady of the amateur dramatics.

(RICHARD *glances at* HELEN *with renewed interest.*)

RICHARD. Are you really ?

HELEN. I play lead . . .

JAMES. Once.

RICHARD. I saw the last show.

JAMES. That's it. She was the one. (*He strikes an attitude as he quotes a line.*) "I do not speak of love. I speak of marriage". Phoo ! What a performance.

RICHARD. I liked it. (*To* HELEN.) Really.

HELEN (*quickly responsive*). Really ?

RICHARD. I did that. (*Still amazed.*) Fancy, now. (*He looks at her, wonderingly.*) I never thought I'd meet you. I—as a matter of fact . . .

HELEN. Yes ?

RICHARD. Well, I never thought you lived round here.

HELEN (*loving the flattery*). Really ? Wherever did you think I lived ?

JAMES. Buckingham Palace, you mug.

RICHARD. I thought. (*He makes a helpless gesture.*) You know . . .

HELEN. Oh, it was nothing.

RICHARD. By gum ! It *is* surprising.

JAMES (*warningly ; out of the side of his mouth*). Aye, aye.

(RICHARD *glances at* JAMES *who jerks a thumb towards the ceiling.*)

Nark it. Nark it. It's her you're taking out, you know.

(HELEN *tries to freeze* JAMES *with a look.*)

HELEN. When you're not being boring you only succeed in being objectionable.

JAMES. Oh ! What play's that out of ?

RICHARD. Are they doing a new one this year ?

HELEN. Yes.

RICHARD. Are you going to be in it?

HELEN. They've asked me. But . . .

JAMES. Why don't you tell him the truth?

HELEN. This conversation doesn't concern you.

JAMES. Oh?

HELEN. No.

JAMES. The play says she's to be seen wearing—

HELEN. Don't listen to him, Mr Sanders.

JAMES. —cami-knickers—and her bloke takes a dim view. They do nothing but row about it. What for I don't know. She's got knock knees, anyway.

HELEN (*furiously*). I have not.

JAMES (*unperturbed*). He's got eyes. Let him have a basinful.

(HELEN *jumps to her feet and lifts her skirts above her knees.* JOAN *enters up* R., *stops a pace in the room and stands patiently, hand on hip.*)

HELEN. Well, Mr Sanders?

JOAN. How long has *this* been going on?

JAMES. Leave 'em alone. They're doing famously.

HELEN. It's his fault. He said I'd got knock knees.

JOAN. Well, you've no need to stand there all night proving it. Cover 'em up. We believe you.

RICHARD (*rising*). Hullo, Joan.

JAMES. Has she got knock knees or hasn't she?

RICHARD. Oh, no.

HELEN. There.

JOAN. I'd like to know what . . . ?

HELEN. Oh, don't be so tiresome, Joan. Mr Sanders and I were talking about the amateur dramatics.

JAMES. And see where it was leading 'em.

RICHARD. You see, my sister Betty was . . .

HELEN. Betty Sanders? She's not your sister?

RICHARD. Oh, yes. She . . .

HELEN. She played Lady in Waiting.

RICHARD. That's right. She . . .

HELEN. She was *wonderful*.

JAMES. They all were—to hear 'em talk.

HELEN. What became of your sister? I never saw her again after the show.

RICHARD. She's back again. Her firm opened an office in London. She had to go there with the boss.

HELEN. Do tell her the new season's just starting. We're just deciding on a play. It might be Shakespeare.

RICHARD. I will. She'll be around.

(JOAN *crosses to the street door and holds it open.*)

JOAN. And I hope you know *I'm* around *and* waiting.

RICHARD (*to* HELEN ; *apologetically*). Well, better be off. Well. Cheerio. (*He moves to the street door.*)

JAMES (*to* HELEN). Thought you weren't going to let her get away with your undies.

JOAN. Why don't you crawl back into your cheese ?

(JOAN *and* RICHARD *exit by the street door. The noise of a motor bike is heard starting up and receding.*)

HELEN (*sitting in the armchair down* L.). Well, I don't know what perverse sort of pleasure you got out of that exhibition. As far as I'm concerned I'd like you to know that I didn't think it was funny.

JAMES. That's because you weren't sitting where I was.

HELEN. There's only one thing I'd like.

JAMES. Carry on.

HELEN. I'd like to be sitting around when you get what's coming to you. Oh ! Wouldn't I just.

JAMES. You'd only just finished having a row with your bloke on the street corner and as soon as Richard Whasisname rolled in and told you how good you were you started to make a pass at him. Women all over. I've got a lot to thank you two for. You've taught me all I want to know about dames. What's more, don't ask me to listen to you reading your dizzy parts any more.

(*As he speaks* HELEN *picks up a book and ostentatiously begins to read.*)

HELEN (*without looking up*). I'm reading.

JAMES. Wasn't that what me and me father were trying to do before you all came in ? A fat lot of studying you can do in this house.

HELEN. So it seems.

JAMES. Is *he* coming round ?

HELEN. Who's he ?

JAMES. Your bloke. Him you're in love with. Him you're always fighting.

HELEN. It might interest you to know that I'm not in love with anybody and I'm having no man telling me what to do and what not to do.

JAMES. Did he give you the air ?

HELEN (*indignantly*). He did not. I'll play what part I like. Why, you'd have thought I was married to him already the way he went on because I might have to appear in scanties.

JAMES. That's the way it goes—love. If he'd have been married to you—long enough mind—you could have walked on the stage naked for all he'd have cared. Trouble is you're too old for him.

HELEN. What d'you mean ?

JAMES. You heard. You know too much. Catch 'em young and tell 'em nothing, not even your name—that's my motto.

HELEN. You stick to your pigeons, my lad. It's safer. (*She puts the book aside.*) I think I'll have my tea after all.

JAMES. Aye, and that poor mug'll be thinking you're too heart-broken to eat.

(HELEN *rises and opens the oven.*)

And there you go—stuffing your innards.

HELEN (*taking her meal from the oven*). You have the most elegant expressions, haven't you ?

JAMES. You'll find it in the dictionary—and you seem to understand them, anyway.

HELEN. I'd be pretty dumb if I didn't—living in the same house with you. (*Suddenly dramatic.*) Heavens ! If only I could be alone.

JAMES. Only one place in this house where you can do that. Dad got there first.

(HELEN *puts her meal on the table at the left end of it, sits and resumes studying while eating.* JAMES *yawns.*)

HELEN. Pass the salt, please.

(*Without looking up,* JAMES *gropes on the table top until he finds the salt cellar which he planks in front of her.* HELEN *tries twice to balance the book against the sugar basin, then exasperatedly puts it aside.*)

(*After a ruminative pause.*) Our Joan's a funny girl, isn't she ?

JAMES. Thought you were studying.

HELEN. I'm eating, aren't I ? It's about time somebody set an example in manners in this house—reading at meals.

JAMES. All right. All right. What's up with our Joan ?

HELEN. It's the fellows she goes out with.

JAMES. What's up with 'em ?

HELEN. The young man who just came in.

JAMES. There was nothing wrong with him as far as I could see. Except that he needs his head examinin' for going out with girls at all. Him with a motor bike, too. What a mug.

HELEN. He's certainly not our Joan's type. Sam Balcombe's more in her line.

JAMES. Oh ?

HELEN. What do you mean "Oh" ?

JAMES. What I say. Just "Oh".

HELEN. Oh.

JAMES. Aye. Oh.

HELEN. I suppose your low mind is thinking I mean he's my type.

JAMES (*broadly sarcastic*). Oh, no.

HELEN. He's got appreciation of finer things than mere jazzing.

JAMES. Like seeing you on the stage.

(HELEN *slaps her knife and fork down and picks up the book.*)

HELEN. I can't stand this any longer. (*She rises in desperation and crosses to the staircase door.*)

JAMES. Temper. Temper.

(HELEN *exits up* R. JAMES *sighs and settles to the newspaper. After a few moments he lowers the paper and rises.*)

Oh, aye. Dad. (*He crosses to the door down* R. *and opens it.*) All right, Dad. You can come out now. (*He resumes his seat* R. *of the table, leaving the door open.*)

(MR BLAIR *enters down* R.)

Come in, Dad. Make yourself at home.

PA. I wonder how long for this time ? Where's our Helen ?

JAMES. Upstairs. Wants to be alone.

PA. Has the feller from the Prudential been ?

JAMES. Doesn't come till tomorrow.

PA. That's a blessing. Is kettle full ?

JAMES (*rising, crossing to the fire and lifting the kettle*). Aye. Singing too. You sit yourself there and I'll fetch you the bread-mug. You can steep 'em in that.

PA. Thank you, lad. By gum ! It'll be a relief, it will and all. Been trying to get 'em done for days.

(JAMES *sets the kettle on the fire, crosses and exits down* R. *He re-enters immediately with a big earthenware bread-mug.*)

Set it down in front of the fire, son.

JAMES (*crossing and placing the mug in front of the fire*). Aye. Better get weaving before Ma comes back. She'll play merry hell if she cops you with your feet in here.

(PA *crosses to the fireplace and sits down in front of the mug.* JAMES *crosses and exits* R. *He re-enters with soap, towel and a large enamel mug of cold water.*)

PA. So will our Helen if she comes down stairs. (*He looks at the empty hook at the side of the fireplace.*) Now who the hell's taken my scissors ?

JAMES. One of the two beauties, you can bet.

PA. How the devil can I do my toe nails without 'em ?

(JAMES *stands on the fender and searches the mantelpiece.*)

JAMES. Here they are. (*He puts the scissors on the arm of the chair.*) Take your boots off, Dad, lad. Borax we used to use in the army. Rare stuff for hardening the old feet.

(PA *takes his boots and socks off with an exclamation of relief.*)

PA. New feet, that's what I want, lad. Forty years in the work-shop plays merry hell with 'em.

JAMES (*picking up the kettle*). About time they retired you on pension, if you ask me. (*He is about to pour water into the mug when he stops, removes a loaf of bread from it, puts the loaf on the table and then puts the water into the mug.*)

PA (*tenderly immersing his feet*). Ahhhh ! That's good.

(*There is a knock on the street door.*)

Now who the hell's that ? Just when I'm enjoyin' myself.

JAMES. Leave 'em to me. I'll soon see 'em off.

(*He crosses to the street door and opens it.* SAM BALCOMBE, *without invitation, enters and makes himself at home. He is a flashily dressed young man. He wears a narrow waisted, padded shouldered overcoat ; pointed patent-leather shoes ; flashy shirt, tie and an American style Stetson hat. He has side-whiskers and a clipped moustache. He demeans himself with an air of complete self-assurance. He carries himself with the aggressive guardedness of a man to whom the world is a huge boxing arena where he must practice eternal vigilance lest someone takes advantage of him.*)

SAM (*crossing and standing below the table*). Evenin', Jim. Evenin', Mr Blair. Washin' the poor old feet ? Take no notice of me. Seen Mrs Dorbell ? Heard she was round here. Can't waste time. You know what it is these days. In and out, quick. S.P.Q.R. and don't be caught with your fingers in the gate.

JAMES. Have you left your barrow outside ?

SAM. Barrow ? Gercher ! Retailin's small stuff. Wholesale touch—that's the job. Thank God for rationin', that's what I say. Want a fag ? (*He proffers a cigarette-case but withdraws it before* JAMES *has a chance to take one.*) O.K. Suits me. Aye, don't know what we'd do without rationin'. (*He lights a cigarette for himself.*)

PA. I know.

SAM. What ?

PA. You'd have to settle down to a steady job of work.

SAM. Job o' work ? What d'you think I'm doin' now ? Fillin' in forms for old dames like Mrs Dorbell so's she can get cheap bacca that I sell for her. Dealin' and makin' contacts for the undercounter stuff. Don't you call that work ? Listen, if it wasn't for us the wheels of industry'd have come to a standstill long ago. Ask any bloke what wants the extras. Fills in ten million forms, waits six months and then he doesn't get any. Comes to me with the ready and—no red tape, Blackpool rules, cash on the table and Bob's your uncle. Anythin' you want—any time—just get into touch with your old pal Sam Balcombe and it's as good as yours.

JAMES. We'll live on our ration books, if you don't mind.

SAM. Suits me.

JAMES. It's chaps like you that'll ruin everything.

SAM. Don't be daft man. The more regulations they bring in the better it is for business. Suits me all right.

PA. I know what'd suit you, my lad.

SAM. Aye ?

PA. Aye. Six months' hard.

SAM. Just a minute. Are you havin' a go at me ?

PA (*shaking his head*). I guess it'd be a waste of breath. You served your time to woodcarving like our James and there's empty benches on the Cathedral job where he's working. Don't leave it too late, lad. Pass the towel, James.

(JAMES *passes the towel to* MR BLAIR *who dries a foot.*)

SAM. Where's the big drum and trombones ? Sounds like I'm at a Salvation Army meeting.

PA. I know it's little use o' talking. You youngsters have lost respect and think it's clever. But honest work's something you can't dodge without paying the penalty in the end.

SAM. I'm working, all right.

JAMES. Aye. Dodgineering.

(PA *dries his other foot.*)

SAM. All right, all right, if you want it that way. You said I ought to have six months' hard. I've already done five years hard. The Japs were waiting to welcome us at Singapore. Reception Committee out at the bottom of the gangplank to march us off to a five year stretch sweatin' it out road makin'. An' I used to think of all the rich old dears in England, aye, and the politicians too, living soft in safe hotels on black market stuff and calling us their brave boys if they thought of us at all. Well, I'm bein' nobody's brave boy no more and I told myself then, that if I came out o' that lot, honest work wasn't going to see me no more. Honest work ! What did I get out of that ? Served my time to woodcarvin' then what ? Nobody wanted woodcarvers, so I finished up chair making in a sweat shop. Gercher ! I'm never going to take off my coat no more.

PA. Sam lad, you know your own business best but you might find easy money's the hardest earned in the end.

SAM. Blimey ! I can't stand this. (*He crosses to the street door.*) Where's your Joan.

JAMES. Out. With a new bloke.

SAM. New bloke ? Who is he ? (*He takes a pace forward.*)

JAMES. Feller with a motor bike. Why the interest ?

SAM. But she never told . . . Never mind. Tell her I'll see her again about the nylons. And . . . Oh, *good* night.

(*He exits by the street door.* JAMES *crosses to the window and looks out after* SAM.)

JAMES. Mmm !

Pa. Clean pair o' socks, James.

(James *does not answer.*)

What's up wi' you ? (*He turns and looks at* James.)

James. Eh ?

Pa. I asked you to pass me a clean pair o' socks.

James. Sam ! The fly guy ! Falling for our kid. There's trouble, there, Dad. There's going to be trouble.

Pa. There'll be enough o' that if your Ma comes in an' catches me at this lark.

(*He sees* Mrs Blair *and* Mrs Dorbell *passing the window.*)

Quick, lad. Shift the blooming bread-mug. Here she is.

(James *stares startled through the window.*)

James. By gum ! You're right.

Pa. Quick, lad. Shift it.

James *takes a pair of socks from the top drawer of the chest of drawers, throws them to* Pa, *then picks up the bread-mug and exits hurriedly with it down* R. Pa *quickly dons his socks.* James *re-enters, sits* R. *of the table and he and* Pa *both sit staring innocently at each other as—*

the Curtain *falls*

ACT II

SCENE 1

SCENE.—*The same. Evening, a few days later.*

When the CURTAIN *rises,* JAMES *is seated in the armchair above the fireplace, staring into the fire. He is without his jacket, his shirt sleeves are rolled and his collar and tie hang on the string under the mantelpiece.* JOAN *enters with a rush by the street door and hurriedly discards her coat and the scarf which serves as headwear.*

JOAN (*glancing at the clock on the mantelpiece*).   Look at the time ! He'll be here before I'm ready. Where's Ma ?

(JAMES *does not look up or reply.*)

(*She whistles shrilly by putting her fingers between her teeth.*) Hey ! You !

(JAMES *looks at* JOAN.)

Where's Ma ?

JAMES.   Gone out.

JOAN.   Where ?

JAMES.   Didn't ask her.

JOAN.   Where's Pa ?

JAMES.   Lodge meeting of his union.   And don't ask me where our Helen is, I don't know.

JOAN.   What's up with you ?

JAMES.   Fed up.

JOAN.   What with ?

JAMES.   Dunno.   Just feeling fed up, that's all.   I can feel fed up if I want, can't I ?

JOAN.   Doesn't bother me.

JAMES.   That's all right, then.

JOAN.   I'm going to change. Let Richard in when he comes, won't you ?

JAMES.   Richard who ?

JOAN.   Richard Sanders. You've already met him.

JAMES.   Oh, the dirt track wallah.

JOAN.   He's not.

JAMES.   Well, I'm not here to amuse your blokes. You should have come in earlier if you knew he was coming.

JOAN.   I would have been if I hadn't been stopped by Sam Balcombe.

18

JAMES. Is he after you too ?

JOAN. Never mind that. I'd like to know what went on here when he called a couple of days ago.

JAMES. You would, would you ?

JOAN. He said he wouldn't come round any more to be got at by you and Pa.

JAMES. He can't take it, eh ? If he's still got it on his brain he must have a conscience still.

JOAN. You leave his conscience alone. I want my nylons.

JAMES. You know what *you* want, don't you ?

JOAN. What ?

JAMES. You want nylons.

JOAN. Aw !

(*She stamps to the stairs and exits up them.* JAMES *stares for a moment into nothingness, then sighs and scratches his head.*)

JAMES. Now what the blooming heck can I do tonight ? I've been to the pictures and done my coupons. I don't fancy the pub and the billiard hall's closed for decorations. (*He looks at the clock.*) Dick Barton isn't on till quarter to seven. (*He sighs.*) I'm fed up—and that's about all there is to it. Blooming well fed up. Must be the moon.

(*There is a knock on the street door.* JAMES *rises and goes listlessly to it.*)

(*While walking to the door.*) This'll be him. (*He opens the door and, without looking to see who the visitor is, returns to his chair into which he flops.*) Come in. Make yourself at home.

(BETTY SANDERS, RICHARD'S *sister, enters and stands in the doorway. She is a lovely girl about* HELEN'S *age. She is turned out in excellent taste and obviously takes pride in her appearance.*)

(*After a pause.*) Shut door after you. She'll be ages, yet. Only just gone upstairs to get herself ready. Just like a blooming woman.

BETTY. Excuse me.

(JAMES *slowly turns in his chair, then seeing* BETTY *at the door, rises and stands to face her from where he has risen.*)

JAMES. Oh—I . . . (*Automatically his hand goes to the open neck of his collarless shirt, which he buttons. He then rolls down his shirt sleeves and fastens the cuffs.*)

BETTY. Is Miss Blair in ?

(JAMES *sidles to the string line stretched under the mantelpiece on which his collar and tie are looped. He takes them off the line and puts them on.*)

JAMES. Oh—er—yes. Yes—er . . . Won't you come inside ?

(BETTY *enters and stands* L. *of the table.*)

(*He closes the door.*) I'm . . . I hope you didn't think I was rude just now. Fact is—I was expecting a chap. You know, friend of my sister's. Which do you want ? Helen or Joan ?

BETTY. Joan. I've a message for her.

JAMES. I'll call her down. She's upstairs getting ready.

BETTY. Don't disturb her. My brother asked me to call. Punctured tyre. He'll be a little late.

JAMES. Oh. You're . . . ?

BETTY. Betty Sanders.

JAMES. How do you do ?

BETTY. Very well, thank you.

JAMES. Ay ! I can't forgive myself leaving you standing on the step like that.

BETTY. Please don't mention it.

JAMES. I was thinking, you know. Sit down for a minute, won't you ?

BETTY. Thank you. (*She sits* L. *of the table.*)

JAMES. Have a cigarette ?

BETTY. No thank you. Can't afford it.

JAMES (*sitting in the armchair above the fireplace*). I keep saying I'll chuck it. Need to be a millionaire don't you ?

BETTY. I don't know. I've never been a millionaire.

(JAMES *grins. There is an awkward pause. He self-consciously indicates his shirt sleeves.*)

JAMES. Sorry you caught me in me—I mean—my shirt sleeves. If I'd . . .

BETTY. Didn't you ask me to make myself at home ?

JAMES. Did I ?

BETTY. Yes. When you first opened the door to me.

JAMES. I'm right sorry about that—leaving you standing there, I mean. I thought it was your brother. (*Eagerly.*) I mean, I still want you to make yourself at home.

BETTY. Why don't you, too ?

JAMES. What ?

BETTY. Make yourself at home. Bothering about not having your coat on. You *do* live here, don't you ?

JAMES. You don't mind, then ?

BETTY. Certainly not. I like to see a man act like a man.

JAMES. How do you mean ?

BETTY. Sleeves rolled up. What's your job ?

JAMES. Oh, me ? I'm only a woodcarver—and a cabinet maker.

BETTY. *Only* a woodcarver. Are you ashamed of it ?

JAMES. Ashamed of it ? Of course I'm not.

BETTY. I should think not, too.

JAMES. Served my time at Jefferson's, I did. Learnt my job from some of the best craftsmen in the world. Though our trade was going out. Nobody wanted us. We were all making cheap furniture in sweat shops. And if the Cathedral hadn't been bombed during the war that's what we'd still have been doing.

BETTY. Are you really working on the choir stalls?

JAMES. Yes.

BETTY. What a wonderful job!

JAMES. Think so?

BETTY. Don't you?

JAMES. Oh—you know . . . It's just a job, like.

BETTY. It isn't. Mine's "just a job" as you call it. Do you know how long those choir stalls have been there?

JAMES. Aye, they were fourteenth century work.

BETTY. You're replacing medieval craftsmen's work with your own and you say it's "just a job".

JAMES. Well, it is, isn't it?

BETTY. But your work will be there for centuries after we're gone and forgotten.

JAMES. Aye, I suppose so. But what I'd like is my own shop. Fed up, I am with all this mass produced rubbish you see around. Place of my own, that's what I want so's I could make *good* stuff. I won first prize with a Jacobean style refectory table, you know.

BETTY. Really?

JAMES. Yes. Just when I'd come out of my time, it was. They had it on show in Manchester. Then the war started and I was called up or I bet I'd have been on my own by now.

BETTY. Are you married?

JAMES. Me? Not blooming likely.

BETTY. You sound as though you're against marriage. Are you?

JAMES. Well—er . . .

BETTY. Yes?

JAMES. I've never given it much thought. I suppose if I met the right girl . . .

BETTY. What do you do with your spare time?

JAMES. I—spare time? I—well, there's my football coupons. And I like a game of snooker.

BETTY. You mean to say you waste your time on frivolities like that when you've got a wonderful craft in your fingers?

JAMES. What d'you mean? A fellow wants a change.

BETTY. Didn't you say you wanted to make good things? Didn't you say you wanted to have a business of your own?

JAMES. Yes. Of course I do.

BETTY. Then why don't you start now in your spare time instead of wasting it on snooker?

JAMES. Mmm. Matter of fact, I never thought of it that way.

BETTY. I'll give you a job.

JAMES. Eh?

BETTY. Could you make me a kidney shaped dressing table ?

JAMES. I'll make you one any shape you want.

BETTY. How much—and how long would it take ?

JAMES. Would mahogany do ? You can get that without permit.

BETTY. Yes.

JAMES. Well, there'd be the materials and my time. I'd go with you and you could pick out the timber and pay for it. Then, well, I'd charge you just for my time in making it.

BETTY. I don't want anything shoddy.

JAMES. I don't turn out nowt—I mean—anything that's shoddy.

BETTY. Why are you always correcting yourself ? If you mean "nowt" say "nowt" and if you mean "anything" say "anything".

JAMES. Well, you see—it's . . .

BETTY. Go on.

JAMES. It's talking to you. Were you born round here ?

BETTY. Yes.

JAMES. You don't talk as though you were.

BETTY. Is there anything wrong with that ?

JAMES. Oh, no. I like to hear you talk. You must have been educated. Were you ?

BETTY. Yes. On scholarships. My children are going to have the best chance possible.

JAMES (*unable to conceal his disappointment*). Oh, are you married ?

BETTY. No.

JAMES. But you just said . . .

BETTY. I meant when I have children.

JAMES. Oh, I see. (*He rubs his knees and can scarce conceal his smiles.*) I suppose being in the amateur dramatics helps you—like—in the way you speak.

BETTY. How did you know I was a member ?

JAMES. Your brother said so when he was here last. He was talking to our Helen. She knows you. Are you getting wed ?

BETTY. Not yet awhile. Why ?

JAMES. Oh, you know. The dressing table. Thought you might be preparing.

BETTY. I want one, that's all.

JAMES. What do you do with *your* spare time ?

BETTY. When I fancy the show I go to the theatre. And you've heard of our amateur shows, haven't you ?

JAMES. Yes. I've held the book for our Helen. I . . .

BETTY. What ?

JAMES. I think I'll have a basinful next time.

BETTY. You should join.

JAMES. What ! Me ? (*He laughs.*) I don't know how to act.

BETTY. Everybody who joins doesn't want to act. You could help with the stage carpentering. There's a meeting tomorrow night. Why don't you come along and I'll introduce you to the producer.

JAMES. Will you really ?

BETTY. Certainly. Anybody who's ready to work is welcome.

JAMES. O.K. I will. What's the next show ?

BETTY. Shakespeare, I think. It isn't decided.

JAMES. Oh. Shakespeare.

BETTY. You don't sound enthusiastic. Have you ever seen a Shakespeare play ?

JAMES. Only one of those Ensa shows in the army. We had to go. C.O. said so. Wasn't up to much.

BETTY. Which one was it ?

JAMES. Blessed if I know. Tell you the truth I couldn't make head or tail of it. Course, I suppose you've got to be educated for that sort of thing.

BETTY. If you suppose so then why don't you start educating yourself ? Don't you ever go to the the theatre ?

JAMES. Music hall now and again. And the pictures if I fancy anything. Not with love in it, o' course. Can't stand that.

BETTY. Oh ?

JAMES. It's always the blooming same. She always gets him in the end.

BETTY. *She* gets him ?

JAMES. Aye. *She* gets him though they try to make it look the other way round—to please the blessed women, I suppose.

BETTY. You sound as though you've a grudge. Do you despise women ?

JAMES. I'm careful, that's all.

BETTY. Cowards are careful.

JAMES. Eh ?

BETTY. What do you mean, "Eh" ? I said, cowards are careful.

JAMES. Well, you're the funniest girl I've ever met.

BETTY. What sort of girls are you in the habit of meeting ?

JAMES. Mostly—er—drips. Want to get a feller to keep 'em. Not my kind, anyway.

BETTY. What is your kind ?

JAMES. I don't know.

BETTY. Isn't it about time you started to make up your mind ?

JAMES. What about ?

BETTY. How long are you going to hang on to your mother's apron strings ?

JAMES (*indignantly*). I'll have you know I keep myself.

BETTY. Yes, in another man's house. You're only a lodger here.

JAMES. I am, am I ?

BETTY. Yes. You're dodging the column. You're old enough to have a house of your own.

JAMES. Now listen. Who do *you* live with ?

BETTY. My people—like you do.

JAMES. Why don't *you* shove off and get wed.

BETTY. I will. The minute I find the right man.

JAMES. Maybe I will, too—when I find the right girl. But let me tell you this, she's not going to learn to cook on me. Seven years I served to learn my trade and being a wife's just as skilled. She's going to be able to bake her own bread and when I come home from work my dinner's going to come out of the oven—not out of a tin or from a fish and chip shop.

BETTY. I hope you find her.

JAMES. If I don't I'll do without.

BETTY. And you've no need to turn your nose up at fish and chips. They're very nutritious.

JAMES. When they're made at home they are.

BETTY. If I gave my husband fish and chips they'd come from a shop.

JAMES. Oh, they would, would they ?

BETTY. They would. In case you don't know it the fumes hang.

JAMES. Fumes ? Hang where ?

BETTY. About the house. The curtains.

JAMES. Open the window then and let 'em out.

BETTY. Tell that to your wife.

JAMES. You wait until I get one.

(*They look at each other and burst into laughter.*)

BETTY. I say, I'm awfully sorry.

JAMES. What for ?

BETTY. Behaving like this. I'm a visitor here, you know.

JAMES. Don't worry your head. I enjoyed it.

BETTY (*looking at the clock*). I'll have to go. (*She rises.*) You really will make the dressing table for me ?

JAMES (*rising*). I'll start right away. Yes, and I'll make a drawing so's there'll be no mistake.

BETTY (*moving to the street door*). Thank you.

JAMES (*moving to the street door and opening it*). And if I turn up at the amateur dramatics tomorrow night it'll be all right ?

BETTY. Certainly.

JAMES. Where's it at ?

BETTY. The assembly room at the *Rose and Crown*. Look in at the best bar first. The landlord lets us study our parts there if he isn't busy.

JAMES. What time ?

BETTY. Quarter to seven.

JAMES. I'll be there.

BETTY. I'll be glad to see you. Good night.

JAMES. Good night.

(BETTY *exits by the street door.* JAMES *stands watching her down the street, then closes the door and stands with a dazed look.*)

Whew ! (*He crosses to the mirror over the mantelpiece where he carefully examines his face including both profiles. He begins to hum to himself.*)

(JOAN *enters up* R. *She peeps into the room, then takes a step forward when she sees that* JAMES *is alone. She is not quite ready. She holds a hand mirror and lipstick. She watches* JAMES *for a second, amazed.*)

JOAN. What're *you* gawping at yourself for ?
JAMES (*turning quickly*). Oh. Nothing.
JOAN. Where is he ?
JAMES. Who ?
JOAN. Richard.
JAMES. He hasn't been yet.
JOAN. Who were you talking to ?
JAMES. His sister. She dropped in to say he'd be a few minutes late. Puncture.
JOAN. What was she like ?
JAMES (*shrugging*). Oh, not bad.
JOAN. Mmm !
JAMES. What d'you mean "Mmm" ?
JOAN. Just "Mmm" ! Give me a shout when he comes.

(*She exits up the stairs.*)

JAMES. O.K. O.K. (*He crosses to the sideboard and searches in the drawers.*) Where the dickens is my design book. "Lazy folk and fools, always lose their tools." (*He finds the book.*) Ah, here we are. (*He sits* R. *of the table, opens the book and looks through it.*) Now. Dressing tables. Dressing tables.

(*The sound of a motor bicycle is heard off. It stops.* JAMES *rises and hurries to the street door.*)

This'll be him. (*He flings the door open, beams and speaks with great heartiness.*) Come in, Dick lad. Come right in.

(RICHARD *enters by the street door.*)

Mended the puncture, I see.
RICHARD. Oh, she came then, my sister ?
JAMES. Oh, yes. She came.
RICHARD. It's a wonder she obliged me.
JAMES. Well, she seemed a very nice young lady to me.

(RICHARD *laughs.*)

What's the laughing matter ?
RICHARD. If you lived with her you'd see. Good job you're a woman hater. She's the type to give a wide berth to. Oho. Not half.
JAMES (*crossing and sitting* R. *of the table*). Oh, well, I suppose you could say that of all of 'em if it came to that.
RICHARD (*offering* JAMES *a cigarette*). Have a fag ?
JAMES. Aye. Ta.

(*They light their cigarettes, then* RICHARD *sits above the table.*)

RICHARD. How's your other sister getting on ?

JAMES. Our Helen ?

RICHARD. Aye.

JAMES. He's had it. She saw him off.

RICHARD. Oh.

JAMES. Don't worry. There'll be another mug on the hook before very long. I don't know what they can see in her.

RICHARD. Well, you can't blame any girl for wanting to make the best of herself.

JAMES. Maybe you're right. Er—your sister's given a bit that way, isn't she ?

RICHARD. What way ?

JAMES. Making the best of herself.

RICHARD. I don't know. Never take that much notice of her.

JAMES. What did you say her name was ?

RICHARD. Bessie.

JAMES. I thought I heard our kid say that her name was Betty.

RICHARD. That's what she calls herself. I pity the poor clot who marries her.

JAMES. Why ?

RICHARD. Oh, if she had her way life'd be one long inspection parade. As far as she's concerned you've got to be improving yourself all the blooming time.

JAMES. What's wrong with improving yourself ?

RICHARD. I'll tell you what's wrong with it as far as I'm concerned. *I* want to have a bit of fun now and again.

JAMES. You can have fun while you're improving yourself, can't you ? If you're doing a job you may as well do it properly. Matter of fact . . .

RICHARD. What ?

JAMES. Well, I've just been asked to make a person a special piece of furniture. And I'll tell you this—it's going to be the best job I can turn out.

RICHARD. I'm not talking about your trade. I'd do the same in mine. I'm talking about the way *she* carries on. I wouldn't like to have been one of those A.T.S. rankers under her.

JAMES. Oh, well, I suppose all women are the same at bottom.

RICHARD. What do you mean ?

JAMES. They all want to be the boss. But I can tell you this, I'd never let any woman come the sergeant major over me.

RICHARD. She would.

JAMES. Let her try it on.

RICHARD. Why, are you . . . ?

JAMES. Don't be daft man. I meant if ever I met her again and she tried to boss me around.

RICHARD. Oh.

JAMES. I've had training, you know.

RICHARD. What sort ?

JAMES. With the two beauties who live here. Her upstairs and the other one—the blooming leading lady, our Helen.

RICHARD. She's a jolly good actress.

JAMES. Um. Are you a member of the amateur dramatics ?

RICHARD. I rig up the lights for them.

JAMES. Our kid's asked me to join.

RICHARD. Acting ?

JAMES. Phoo ! No. Acting ? Me ? Don't be daft. Something about stage carpentering.

RICHARD. Are you going to do it ?

JAMES. Well—matter of fact I've not decided. You see, I'll need all the spare time I can get. I'm thinking of starting up on my own.

RICHARD. What as ?

JAMES. Cabinet making, of course. I think I told you—I've just got an order for a dressing table.

RICHARD. Well, you can't go wrong in your trade these days.

(HELEN *enters by the street door. She carries a small brown paper parcel.* RICHARD, *with his back to the door, does not see her.*)

Stick to that and give the sergeant major in skirts a wide berth.

HELEN. Good evening.

RICHARD (*rising and turning*). Oh. Good evening.

(HELEN *removes her hat, puts it on the chest of drawers, goes to the mirror and pats her hair.*)

HELEN. Who's the sergeant major in skirts ?

JAMES. You'd fill the bill.

(HELEN *crosses to the chest of drawers and takes from the drawer a paper pattern, a pair of scissors and a pin box. She puts these, with the brown paper parcel, on the table. She then opens the parcel which contains a length of dress material and spreads it on the table.*)

HELEN. Move your book, please.

JAMES. And what d'you think *you're* going to do ?

HELEN. Cut out this skirt.

JAMES. Not on this table you're not.

HELEN. Don't be mean, now.

JAMES. Use the floor. I want this table to rest my drawing board on.

HELEN. Which drawing board ?

JAMES. What do you mean "Which drawing board" ? *My* drawing board, of course. The one I made.

HELEN. Then you'd better start making another. Mother lent it to Mrs Dorbell.

JAMES. Eh ? What for ?

HELEN. Her table top. Her own had fallen in pieces.

JAMES (*furious*). Well, that's the blooming limit. Wait till I see Ma.

HELEN. Oh, go on, you never used the thing. In any case our Joan's been using it for months to practise her tap dancing on.

(JAMES *rises and stamps to the street door.*)

JAMES. Well, I'm going to get it back. And you'd all better learn to keep your maulers off my things in this house or there'll be trouble.

(JAMES *exits muttering and slams the door.* HELEN *lays the material on the table and pins the pattern to it.*)

HELEN. Just like him. Used it once in a blue moon—leaves it in everybody's way, then expects it to be there when he wants it. Where are you off tonight ?

RICHARD. Oh, you know. Just the usual. A spin out. Er . . .

HELEN. Yes ?

RICHARD. It's—they're—the amateur dramatics are starting up again. Are you coming ?

HELEN. Yes.

RICHARD. Oh. I'm glad of that.

HELEN. Are you ? Why ?

RICHARD. Oh, well. I just . . . You know. Just . . . Well, now that I know you it'll make the reunion party all the more interesting. I've taken on the electrician's job, you know.

HELEN. Fine. Is Betty joining again ?

RICHARD. I suppose so. She was round here tonight.

HELEN. Here ? What for ?

RICHARD. I'd had a puncture. She came round to tell Joan I'd be late. Seems she talked James into joining the dramatics.

HELEN. Our James ! (*She laughs.*) And what the dickens does *he* think he'll be able to do ?

RICHARD. Stage carpentering, I think.

HELEN. Your Betty came here—and then our James is going to join the dramatics, eh ? Oho !

RICHARD. It looks that way, doesn't it ?

HELEN. It certainly does. (*She unpins the paper pattern and now tries it for length.*) Would you mind giving me a hand ? (*She stands down* C.)

RICHARD (*moving to* HELEN). Certainly.

HELEN. It's a little too long. There are the pins. I want it shortening by an inch.

RICHARD. Shall I fold it back and pin it ? That the idea ?

HELEN. That's it. You'll do it better if you kneel.

RICHARD. Yes. I think I would. (*He kneels and awkwardly begins to pin the pattern.*)

(JOAN *enters up* R., *stops, stares, then approaches quietly and stands behind them.*)

JOAN. And what's the idea *this* time ?

RICHARD (*rising*). I was just . . .

JOAN. I know. I know. It was knees last time : now you've got him giving you a fitting. You're getting on. You're getting on.

(HELEN *gives* JOAN *a crushing look, then turns to* RICHARD *with a charming smile.*)

HELEN. I'm sorry my sister's chosen to behave this way, Mr Sanders. Thanks for helping me.

JOAN. And the lah-di-dah doesn't cut any ice with me, either. I'm ready, Dick.

(JAMES *enters from the street. He flings the door open and stands glaring at* JOAN *with a thunderous expression on his face. He carries a large drawing board, whose surface has been ruined by flat-iron scorches and other signs of careless housekeeping. He leaves the door open to reveal* SAM, *who stands in the doorway.* JAMES *displays the board.*)

JAMES (*accusingly*). Look ! Just look at this. My drawing board. See that ? And that ? They're heel marks—tap dancing. *You* did that. (*He puts the board on the table.*)

JOAN. What of it ? This is a house—not a workshop.

JAMES (*wagging a forefinger*). Let me catch you mucking about with it again and there'll be trouble.

JOAN. That'll be something new in this house, won't it ? (*She sees* SAM.) And what's the matter with honest Sam ?

(SAM *enters.*)

SAM. You *are* going out, then.

JOAN. Does it look as though I'm going to bed ?

SAM. I've had enough of this.

JAMES. What is all this ?

HELEN. I should say it's something that doesn't concern you.

(SAM *glares at* RICHARD.)

SAM. No. But it concerns him.

RICHARD. Who is this chap ?

SAM. Somebody who can take care of himself, chum.

JOAN. Sam Balcombe—don't you dare.

RICHARD. I don't know who you are, but, look . . .

(JAMES *turns the chair above the table, ostentatiously seats himself, folds his arms and settles comfortably.*)

JAMES. This is it. Get the gloves on. Over a blooming woman, too.

SAM. And I don't know who you are . . .

JOAN. Well, you both know who *I* am.

JAMES. Not half. The woman men can't resist. The kiss of death. *You* would spoil it. (*He rises.*) Well, pardon me, folks, I'm going to have a basinful of Dick Barton. (*He crosses to the radio.*)

SAM. I want to know where I stand, Joan Blair.

(MRS DORBELL *enters from the street. She halts in the doorway.*)

JOAN. If you think you can barge in here any time you like and try to show me up in front of friends you're jolly well mistaken.

RICHARD. Do you want me to chuck him out ?

SAM. Come and try it on.

(MRS DORBELL *moves above the table.*)

MRS DORBELL. Hullo. Hullo.

JAMES. Quiet, Nancy. You're interrupting a row.

MRS DORBELL. That's a thing I've never done in my life. I enjoy 'em too much. I think I'll make myself at home. You don't meet with this kind of entertainment private every day.

JOAN. Go on, Nancy. Hop it.

MRS DORBELL. I could hear just as well from the front door but it's more comfortable here. (*She sits above the table.*) I'm not shiftin' from here.

(MR BLAIR *enters from the street and stands just inside the door.*)

SAM (*pointing to* RICHARD). And *she's* not going out with him.

PA. Who's not going out with who ? And what's going on here ? So, it's you again causing trouble, Sam Balcombe.

SAM. Aye, it's me again. And I want an understanding.

PA. It's not the only thing you want.

JOAN. And he's come to the right place to get it.

(HELEN *shifts the drawing board from the table, and leans it against the sideboard.*)

HELEN. This thing's in my way, our James.

MRS DORBELL. My God ! My table top ! What's that doin' here ?

JAMES. It's my drawing board. I'll have to make you a table top.

PA. Listen, all of you. Whose house d'you think this is ?

MRS DORBELL. Landlord's, love.

SAM. For the last time, Joan Blair. Are you coming with me ?

JAMES. Where're you thinking of taking her ? (*He switches on the radio.*)

SAM. If it's any of your business I've got passages to South Africa. (*To* JOAN.) Are you coming ?

JOAN. No.

SAM. Why ?

RICHARD. She said "No". Isn't that enough ?

SAM. It's enough from you. Are you looking for a black eye ?

RICHARD. No. Why, lost one ?

To face page 31—" Too Clever for Love "

SAM (*furiously*). That's enough. Come on. Outside.

JAMES. Now we're getting somewhere.

RICHARD. Anything to oblige.

(SAM *stamps to the street door, dragging his coat off, and exits.* RICHARD
follows him off.)

JOAN. I'll never speak to you again, Sam Balcombe.

RADIO ANNOUNCER. The time is six forty five. This is the
B.B.C. Light Programme.

JAMES. It *would be*—just at this time.

SECOND ANNOUNCER. Dick Barton. Special Agent.

(*The Dick Barton music,* "*The Devil's Gallop*" *commences on the
radio.* JOAN *rushes to the street door.* JAMES *follows* JOAN *and they
look out into the street.* MRS DORBELL *rises and pushes between*
JOAN *and* JAMES. PA *flops into the chair above the fireplace, sighs
and looks at the ceiling.*)

JOAN. They're fighting. They're fighting. Stop them.

JAMES (*stepping into the street*). Go on, Dick lad, your left. Your
left.

The Dick Barton music rises to a crescendo as—

the CURTAIN *falls*

SCENE 2

SCENE.—*The "Best Room" of the "Rose and Crown". The following
evening.*

It is a smallish and comfortable room panelled in mahogany.
A door L. leads to the other bars and the main entrance. A door up R.
leads to a corridor and stairs to the assembly room above. The bar
counter, in the form of a large hatch is L.C. of the back wall, and is
fitted with beer pump handles. Shelves behind the bar are well
stocked with the usual bottles of spirits, beers and minerals.
Sundry advertisements for cigarettes, beers and spirits adorn the
walls. A long settle stands against the back wall R. of the bar. There
is a small circular table down L. and another R. with three chairs
set to it. A piece of carpet and a spittoon on the floor complete the
furnishings.

(*See the Ground Plan and Photograph of the Scene.*)

When the CURTAIN rises, TOM HOLROYD, the landlord, is behind the
bar, leaning on it and reading a newspaper. He is a big-paunched
man, an ex-England Rugby League International. He is a jovial
fellow who enjoys life, though the present depressing state of trade in
the public house business tries his good nature considerably. MRS
DORBELL is standing at the table R., dusting it.

MRS DORBELL. Waste o' time, if you ask me.

TOM. Eh ?

MRS DORBELL. This dustin'. Waste o' time, I said.

TOM. Why ?

MRS DORBELL. Nobody's got the money.

TOM. Now what the 'ell are you on about ?

MRS DORBELL. This room.

TOM. What's up with it ?

MRS DORBELL. What I've just told you. Nobody's got the money now the war's over to pay the prices you charge for drinks in here. You'd do better to close this room down till the next war starts and the Yanks come back.

TOM. That doesn't look as though it's far off, either.

(MRS DORBELL *pauses in her job, transfixed by remembrance of American generosity.*)

MRS DORBELL. Never a night passed but what one of 'em bought me a double.

TOM. Who ?

MRS DORBELL. Those American and Canadian lads, o' course. Souls o' generosity, that's what they were.

TOM. Aye, those were the days. Plenty o' brass flyin' around then.

MRS DORBELL. It flew past me, all right. Expectin' somebody ? (*She moves to the settle.*)

TOM. Where ?

MRS DORBELL. Here. Havin' me dustin' it out. What's this ? (*She indicates a roll tool-kit on the settle.*)

TOM. Belongs the lad that looks after the electric side of those amateur theatricals. It's their rehearsal night upstairs.

MRS DORBELL. Oh. Them.

TOM. Aye, this room'll be full of 'em learnin' their parts and mutterin' to 'emselves. An' another thing, Nancy.

(MRS DORBELL *looks at* TOM.)

It's no use you hangin' around thinkin' they'll buy you a drink.

MRS DORBELL. Cadgin' drinks ? Me ?

TOM. You'll be wastin' your time. They're what they call intellectuals an' you've never found one o' them with sixpence to scratch 'emselves with.

MRS DORBELL. If it comes to that I've not got sixpence to scratch myself with and I'm no blooming intellectual.

(JAMES *enters* L. *He wears his Sunday best. He stands in the doorway grinning and shy.*)

Hello, James Blair, an' what're you doin' here ?

JAMES. Evenin', Nancy. Evenin', Tom.

TOM. Evenin'.

Mrs Dorbell.　Got his Sunday clothes on, he has.

James.　Well, I haven't got to fill in a form to put those on now, have I ?

Mrs Dorbell.　When a young feller starts wearin' *them* in the middle o' the week there's usually a wench on the scene.

James.　Is there, now ?

Mrs Dorbell.　Aye, there is there, now.

(James *crosses to the bar and stands* R. *of it*.)

James.　If you must know I've been asked to join the amateur theatricals.

Tom.　What'll it be, James.　The usual ?

James.　I'll have a ginger beer while I'm waiting.

(Tom *and* Mrs Dorbell *stare*.)

Tom.　Did you say "Ginger beer" ?

James.　Yes.

Tom.　What'll you have with it ?

James.　Ginger beer.　Just ginger beer.　And there's no need to stare.　It seems a fellow can't do what he wants or have what he wants nowadays.

Mrs Dorbell.　Sunday suit and ginger beer, eh ?

James.　Aye, Sunday suit—and ginger beer, if you don't mind.

Tom (*serving the drink with a wry face*).　Don't know how you can sup the stuff.

Mrs Dorbell.　Pint o' the best'd do you more good.

Tom.　That it would.

James.　Look what it's done to you.

Tom.　What's up wi' me ?

James.　Look at the size o' the belly you've got.

Tom.　I'm just well made, that's all.

Mrs Dorbell.　Go on, you're as fat as a miller's pig.

James.　You could have bought a Rolls Royce with what it cost you to get that.

(Tom *proudly and lovingly strokes his curves*.)

Tom.　I'd rather have this.　If I'd a Rolls Royce and died somebody else'd get it.　But this is mine—and when I die I take it with me.

Mrs Dorbell.　Aye, an' when you do go, lad, somebody else'll have to carry it to where it's goin'.

Tom.　You're right, Nancy.　And you deserve a drink.

James.　But will she get it ?

Mrs Dorbell.　I've deserved a lot o' things in my time but few have come my way.

Tom (*drawing a pint of beer*).　There you are, love.　There's one that did.　I'm doin' well tonight.　One customer in at six o'clock for half o' mild, James there on ginger beer an' now here's me *givin'* it away.

MRS DORBELL (*toasting* TOM). Never mind, love, you'll get your reward. (*To* JAMES.) What d'you keep startin' at the door for ? Expectin' somebody ?

JAMES. If you must know I'm expectin' the chap that goes out with my sister.

MRS DORBELL. Him that was fightin' ?

TOM. Who was he fightin' ?

MRS DORBELL. Honest Sam. Sam Balcombe.

(SAM *enters* L. *He has a black eye and wears his best "spiv" suit.*)

SAM. Well ? What're you all gawping at ?

MRS DORBELL. He's got *his* Sunday suit on, too.

JAMES. When you're spivvin' it's Sunday every day.

TOM. What're *you* dolled up for, Sam ?

MRS DORBELL. What did you get dolled up for when you were his age ?

TOM (*laughing*). Eh, Nancy, that was a long time ago. Though I'm not played out yet, remember.

MRS DORBELL. No use lookin' at me. (*She raises her glass.*) This is my pastime now.

(SAM *grunts impatiently.*)

TOM. What'll it be, Sam ?

SAM (*crossing and standing* L. *of the bar*). Give us a ginger beer.

TOM. This is catching. What's up with you ?

SAM. Nothing. It's her. Won't talk to me if she smells even a half pint on my breath.

TOM. Well, I'll be damned glad when you're all wed an' got it out of your system—then you can come back to a civilized way of living. (*He mutters as he opens a ginger beer.*) Blooming ginger beer. More like an ice cream shop.

MRS DORBELL. Marriage. Puh !

SAM. And what's wrong with marriage ?

MRS DORBELL. There's nothing like trying it to find out.

TOM. And you're dead right there, Nancy.

SAM. You know nothing about it. You never got wed.

TOM. Didn't get hanged, either, but I've got my ideas about it just the same.

JAMES. He'll tell you you never met the right girl in a minute, Tom.

TOM. Never met the wrong one, either. It was bad enough when you could get a proper house of your own. But—love in a pre-fab.

MRS DORBELL. Pre-fab ? Don't be daft. You need influence and a string o' kids before you can get one o' them. Caravans, what you can't swing a cat in, that's what they're goin' in for now.

JAMES. Even they come in handy when the bums are after you.

SAM. Well, I'm goin' in no pre-fab—nor a caravan. I know my way around.

JAMES. Any lad who finds he's being led to the altar doesn't know his way around.

TOM. You're right there, James.

SAM. Fat lot either of you know about it.

TOM. Stand behind this bar for a couple o' weeks an' listen to the married 'uns talk—male *and* female—and you'll hear enough to be goin' on with.

JAMES. The way he talks you'd think he'd already got a blooming house.

SAM. I know when to keep this shut. (*He touches his lips.*)

JAMES. Thought you were all for emigrating to South Africa.

SAM. You know what thought did.

MRS DORBELL. When you're in love like he is you aren't capable of thinking.

TOM. You can see that by the colour of his eye.

SAM. What's wrong with my eye?

TOM. Nothin' at all—if you like it that colour.

SAM. You should see the other feller's.

JAMES. We will. He'll be here directly.

MRS DORBELL (*shaking her head*). We never learn, Tom, lad— until it's too late.

TOM. What's up now, love?

MRS DORBELL. You wouldn't believe it, Sam, but a couple of young men had a fight over me when I was a lass. Take a good look. Who'd fight over me now?

TOM. I would. If I heard anybody sayin' anything against you I'd fetch him one across the chops.

MRS DORBELL. Bless you, lad. That's different, though, and you know it.

JAMES. What's on your mind, Nancy?

MRS DORBELL. The same as'd be on yours if you'd been born in the country like me. Bringin' little children into a world like this. Green fields all round when . . .

SAM. We know. An' now queues miles long for houses : pre-fabs in the public park. We've heard you before. Well, if I want to get wed and have a family I don't care how many people there are in the world. Mine won't go short. I'll see to that.

JAMES (*winking at* TOM). Going to make an uncle out of me—he hopes. That's if he's lucky. Her ladyship might have other ideas. D'you know Richard Sanders?

TOM. Don't think so.

JAMES. In a regular job of work, he is. Good looking fellow, too.

SAM. He won't be if he comes my way.

JAMES. Should be here any minute now.

MRS DORBELL (*putting her drink on the bar*). Well, I've come here to enjoy myself and I don't want my beer knocked over with your

fighting. Pass it through into the other bar, Tom where there'll be
a bit o' peace and quiet. (*She mutters as she crosses to* L.) **Fightin'!**
Pity they've nothin' better to do with their time.

(*She exits* L., *leaving her purse on the settle.* TOM *passes her beer
to the other bar, returns and picks up a spiling mallet from under
the counter.*)

TOM. And talking about fighting. Before anybody starts that
lark in here—remember this. (*He raps the bar top.*) The old pacifier.

(*He exits behind the bar.*)

JAMES (*singing softly*).
                "No cares have I to grieve me,
                    No pretty little girls to deceive me ... "
SAM. Aw. Pipe down.
JAMES. Always looking for trouble, aren't you? Honest Sam,
the wide guy. One minute tickets to South Africa for you and our
kid, the next you've got a house.
SAM. Who said I'd got a house?
JAMES. Don't know and don't care. I'll tip you off with one
thing, though.
SAM. What's that?
JAMES. If it hasn't got a bath in it you'll be wasting your time
with her.
SAM. You needn't worry about that. It has.
JAMES. I'm not worrying. Count me out of the matrimonial
stakes. Another thing.
SAM. What?
JAMES. While you're in the spiv racket you won't be racing with
her.
SAM (*gloomily*). That's the trouble—not knowing where I stand.

(SAM *takes his hat off and absently scratches his head.* JAMES *leans
forward towards him furtively on tip-toe and glances at his crown.*
SAM *notices the movement and looks at him suspiciously.* JAMES
cocks his glance at the ceiling and begins to whistle.)

(*Suspiciously.*) What were you squinting at?
JAMES. Oh—just wondering.
SAM. What about?
JAMES. Are you really going bald?
SAM (*taken aback*). Eh?
JAMES. You heard.
SAM (*amazed*). Bald? Me? (*Indignantly.*) Have a look for
yourself. (*He stoops in front of* JAMES *and shows his crown.*)

(JAMES *carefully examines* SAM'S *head.*)

JAMES (*dubiously*). Well, I dunno. Matter of opinion, I suppose.
SAM. Am I or amn't I?

JAMES. You *are* getting a bit thin on the top. Still, Sam, none of us're getting any younger. Pooh! What the 'ell have you got on it? You smell like a jessie. Is it to cure it?

SAM. Is what to cure what?

JAMES. The stuff you put on—curing the bald spot?

SAM (*shouting ; furiously*). But I haven't got a bald spot.

JAMES. Have a look.

SAM. Don't talk so flamin' daft. How can I?

JAMES. Then how d'you know? Are you worried about anything?

SAM. Course I am. You know I am.

JAMES. P'raps it's that that's the cause of it. Try massage. D'you read those advertisements? You know—"Thin on top now? How will you look at forty?"

(SAM *feels for the imagined bald spot.*)

SAM. Is it really, though?

JAMES. Aw, stop fretting, man. That's the trouble with you where our Joan's concerned. You're pressing too much.

SAM (*still with his fingers on his crown*). But did she really say I was going bald?

JAMES. No names no pack drill, you know that. I could mark your card for you if I liked. You're not all that bad.

SAM. Would you, though?

JAMES. Might do. Trouble with you is you don't use your head.

SAM. Don't be daft. How d'you think I got my dough? And if it comes to motor bikes—don't you forget it, I could get a car if I wanted.

JAMES. We know that. But it's our Joan you want, not a car.

SAM. It'll be a padded cell in the looney bin I'll want if this goes on much longer. It's driving me bald headed.

JAMES. I've just told you it's started going thin on top. But you've nobody but yourself to blame. Because you've a pocketful of dough you think it'll buy anything.

SAM (*indignantly*). D—d—d'you mean . . . ? Are you suggesting that I think money'd buy your . . . Why! I'll knock your clock round if . . .

(TOM *enters behind the bar, produces the mallet, looks at* SAM *and gives the bar top a solitary knock. He nods at* SAM, *replaces the mallet, nods again and exits.*)

JAMES. See. It's found you out.

SAM. What has?

JAMES. The spivving you're up to the neck in. It's made you suspicious of everybody.

SAM. And what am I suspicious about now?

JAMES. For one thing—that blessed house. You're so cagey about it you'd think *I* was after the blooming thing. I'm not courting and no intentions, neither. Leave that to mugs like you and the lad with the motor bike.

SAM. I trust nobody.

JAMES. Just what I've said. And where's it getting you with our Joan except that black eye?

SAM. Leave my eye out of it.

JAMES. It's Richard Sanders' fist you ought to have left out of it.

SAM. If he comes into this pub tonight I'll knock seven sorts out of him.

(TOM *peers round the hatch at* SAM.)

TOM. I can hear you.

(*He withdraws his head.*)

JAMES. Hopeless, that's what you are. I'm the mug for trying to help you.

SAM. Why should you want to help me?

JAMES (*crossing and sitting* L. *of the table* R.). You're in the British Legion, too, aren't you? We believe in helping. Besides, I like to see a lad happy.

SAM. How d'you reckon to do it?

JAMES. I could put a good word in for you with our kid, couldn't I?

SAM. Would you?

JAMES. If you were on the level, I might. Have you bought that house you were talking about?

SAM (*crossing and sitting* R. *of the table* R.). Course I haven't. What's the use of doing that till I know where I stand? The old woman who owns it'll sell if only your Joan'll make up her mind whether she'll have me or not. If she doesn't say so quick the old woman'll sell to somebody else.

JAMES. I should have thought a clever lad like you wouldn't have had much trouble in selling it again—at a profit. That's if our Joan turns you down—as seems likely.

SAM (*anxiously*). D'you think she will? Really?

JAMES. That's up to you, isn't it? Any case, I think you're daft wanting to get wed. I'll do what I can. But I've told you already that it'll be no good, that house, if it hasn't got a bath.

SAM (*irritably*). It's got a flaming bath. I've already told you.

JAMES. Aye, an' so has ours. But it's on a nail on the backyard wall.

SAM. This a proper 'un—in a bathroom. *And* the house has got a garden back and front. *And* a garage.

JAMES. I'll believe it when I see it.

SAM. I'll take you round and show it to you. I'll call for you at the Cathedral. What time?

JAMES. We knock off at five. And while you're there it wouldn't be a bad idea if you met the foreman. I'm telling our Joan no lies, you know.

SAM (*incredulously*). You're wanting me to go back to work?

JAMES. Look, Sam, an' get this into your bald head. As far as I'm concerned you can jump into the cut. It's our Joan.

(SAM *stares thoughtfully at the floor.*)

SAM. I wish I knew whether she's going to have me.

JAMES. I know you do and I can't understand it. The fly guy falling for marriage. Why d'you want to change things ? You're doing all right as you are, aren't you ?

SAM (*heaving a great sigh*). No. Can't sleep for thinking about her. I think I'd go batty if anybody else got her. (*Snappily*.) And I don't want any wisecracks from you. There it is and there's nothing I can do about it. You be glad you've fallen for nobody.

JAMES. I've no complaints. Love, eh ?

SAM. Aye, love.

(*Both sigh and stare at the floor. The silence that ensues attracts* TOM's *attention. He pokes his head into the bar and looks at them.*)

TOM. And what's up wi' you two ?

JAMES. We're thinkin'.

(TOM *enters and stands behind the bar.*)

TOM. So would I be if I was suppin' that rot-gut you've got in front of you. A good pint o' beer down the both o' you and you'd have somethin' cheerful to think about.

SAM. Are you on the water waggon too ?

TOM. Ginger beer waggon, that's what he's on.

JAMES. I do my drinkin' after I've done my business.

SAM. What business is this ?

JAMES. It *was* supposed to be private and confidential, but as it's all fair, square and above board I don't mind who knows. They want me in the amateur theatricals and I'm thinkin' of starting up in business on my own.

SAM. What ? Acting ?

JAMES. Don't be daft.

SAM. What sort of business, then ?

JAMES. Cabinet making—for them as 're tired of rubbish and want to pay extra for a good job of work.

SAM. An' where d'you reckon your going for your customers ?

JAMES. Nowhere. They're comin' to me.

SAM. When ?

JAMES. Started already.

SAM. You mean you've got some orders ?

JAMES. I do. I'll put you down for a bedroom suite if you like. Got my eye on some lovely Spanish walnut. Now, if you'd give me the order I could let it drop, casual like, to our Joan, that you were thinkin' of gettin' wed.

SAM. Aren't you forgetting something ? I'm a cabinet maker and a woodcarver, too.

JAMES. If you were you'd be standin' a chance with our Joan.

TOM. Ay, deary me. Here's a lad, free as a bird, picking up a packet on the fiddle and he's ready to go back to honest work at three an' two an hour—all for love. (*He shakes his head and turns to go.*) Ay, deary me. Deary me.

(*He exits behind the bar.*)

JAMES. There's a hell of a lot in what he says, Sam.

SAM. You wait until you fall. And we'll see whether you'll be able to see straight. (*Aloud to himself.*) Me, the wide guy ! Feelin' as though I'll cry me eyes out if she turns me down.

JAMES (*holding out his handkerchief*). There you are. In there.

SAM. Oh, go to hell. You don't understand.

(*Both reach for their glasses and both drink.* SAM *belches.*)

JAMES. Granted.

SAM. Pardon me. It's this stuff.

(*They both stare thoughtfully at the floor. Their silence again attracts the attention of* TOM *who enters behind the bar and looks at them. The sound of hurried footsteps off* R. *engages the attention of* JAMES *and* SAM *who both turn and look hopefully at the door* R. BETTY *enters* R. JAMES *rises.*)

BETTY (*to* JAMES). Oh, hello.

JAMES (*beaming*). Hello. I've—er—come.

BETTY (*to* TOM). Has Aubrey been, Mr Holroyd ?

TOM. Aubrey ? Who's Aubrey ?

BETTY. You know. Tall, fair-haired, good-looking . . .

TOM. I've seen no Aubrey. You seen him, James ?

JAMES (*jealously*). No good-looking fellers been in since I've been here.

BETTY (*frowning impatiently*). I wish people would appear on time. (*To* JAMES.) Why didn't you come up to the rehearsal room ?

JAMES. I didn't know anybody was there.

BETTY. Your Joan's up there—with Richard.

SAM (*rising*). She is, is she ? How long has she been there ? I've been waiting.

BETTY. Will you come up or shall I tell her you're here ?

SAM. Tell her I'm here. I want that feller she's with kept out of my way.

(JAMES *crosses to the door* R. *and stands aside.*)

BETTY. This way, Mr Blair.

(*He exits* R.)

JAMES (*to* TOM). Aubrey ! What a name. Well, here's me for the scenery bashing.

(*He exits* R.)

SAM (*oblivious of* TOM).   I know who I'd like to bash.

(TOM *shakes his head despairingly.*)

Blimey !

(SAM *scratches the back of his neck and his fingers wander to the crown of his head, then, seeing the mirror over the settle, he crosses to it and attempts the impossible of trying to inspect the imagined bald spot.* TOM *regards him stolidly.* SAM *glances expectantly at the door* R., *then quickly smooths his hair, straightens his tie and sits* R. *of the table* R. BETTY *and* JOAN *enter* R. BETTY *carries a "Temple Shakespeare".* SAM *stares disapprovingly when he sees* BETTY.)

SAM.   Oh.

JOAN.   And what's the "Oh" for ?

SAM.   I wanted to talk to you alone.

JOAN.   And what if I didn't want to talk to you alone ?

(TOM *shakes his head and exits behind the bar.*)

BETTY.   Don't take any notice of me.   I'm studying my part.
(*She crosses to the bar and opens her book.*)

JOAN.   Why did you come here ?

SAM.   Aw—love.

JOAN.   Don't "love" me.

(BETTY *begins to pace to and fro at the bar concentrating as she murmurs and memorizes her lines.*)

SAM.   But I do.   Can't help it.
O, Joan, Joan, I'd do anything
for you.   Anything.

JOAN.   Then catch that boat to
South Africa.

SAM.   Like a shot, if you'll
come.

JOAN.   I'm staying where I am.

SAM.   Won't you change your
mind ?

JOAN.   Never.

BETTY.   "Feed him with apricocks
and dewberries,
With purple grapes, green
figs and mulberries ;
The honey bags steal
from the humble-bees,
And for night-tapers crop
their waxen thighs,
And light them at the
fiery glow-worm's eyes,
To have my love to
bed . . ."

SAM (*rising*).   Oh, how the hell can we talk !   (*He points at* BETTY.)
Her and her bumble bees.

BETTY.   Sorry if I'm in the way.

JOAN.   There's only one person in the way and he knows who it is.

BETTY (*crossing to the door* R.).   The corridor will do for me just as
well.

(*She exits* R. SAM *sits and stares dejectedly at the floor.*)

SAM. Pity I ever came back. Don't know where I'm going,
I don't. Always at me you are, an' you don't understand that it
was only you that kept me going when there was nothing to live for.

JOAN. Why pick on me ?

SAM. All the pals I had and all the girls I knew—you were the
only one that sent me a letter to the prison camp.

JOAN. Go on. Perhaps mine was the only one that got through.

SAM. It did though, didn't it ? I could recite it now—backwards.
I read it and re-read it until it fell in pieces. Then there was the
other thing.

JOAN. What ?

SAM. The day I left. The last day of my draft leave. You
kissed me.

JOAN. Did I ?

SAM. Oh, don't tell me you've forgotten. Oh, don't say that.

JOAN. No, I remember.

SAM (*challengingly*). Where was it, then ?

JOAN. Near the telephone pole in North Street.

SAM. It was that—and your letter that kept me sane. There's
only one girl in all the world for me and that's you. Now tell me to
go.

(JOAN *crosses to* SAM *and speaks on a note of tenderness.*)

JOAN. Come on, Sam. Pull your socks up.

SAM. It's not your sympathy I want. All the deals I've done and
all the money I've earned—it was all for you. Aye, you can look at
me. It's true. I've had enough of going without things. I wanted
you to want for nothing.

JOAN. You'd have done yourself more good by me if you'd offered
me a wage packet.

SAM. If I could be sure there was a . . .

JOAN. You can't be sure of anything in this world. And stop
leaning on me. You've got a backbone. Lean on that.

(SAM *rises with an air of determination.*)

SAM. I'll go back to work.

JOAN. That'll be a start in the right direction, anyway.

SAM. I've already made the start. I'm meeting your James at the
Cathedral tomorrow and I'm seeing the foreman. I can get a job
any time at Jefferson's on the Cathedral.

JOAN. Any time's no time.

SAM. I've told you. Tomorrow. Five o'clock. (*Pleadingly.*)
Will you come with me ?

JOAN. Where ?

SAM. A walk. Now. (*Ingratiating.*) Please, Joan. I want to
talk to you.

JOAN. What about ?

SAM. Well, for one thing (*impatiently*) there's the blooming money. You said I didn't get it honest. What have I got to do with it ?

JOAN. You can start by buying yourself a pair of working overalls.

SAM. I can't do that until the shops open in the morning, can I ? Besides, I'm talking about money. Big money. (*Warningly*.) I'm not giving it to the poor. Your children's going to have . . .

(RICHARD *enters* R. *He is without his coat and his sleeves are rolled up. He carries a screwdriver. He, too, has a black eye.*)

JOAN. Just a minute, Sam Balcombe. Just a minute. You be certain you're going to be the father of my children before you start making plans for them.

RICHARD. Hallo. You here again ?

SAM. Listen, chum. If you'd like another shiner to go with the one you've got already . . .

JOAN. At it again, Sam Balcombe.

(TOM *enters behind the bar.* SAM *mumbles something.*)

JOAN. What did you say ?

SAM. All right. All right. I'm sorry.

RICHARD. If I'm butting in, Joan . . .

JOAN. Nobody's butting in on anything.

RICHARD. Excuse me. I'm holding up the job. Where's the main fuse box, Tom ?

TOM. Cupboard. Top of the stairs.

RICHARD. Thanks.

(*He exits* R.)

TOM (*indicating the mallet*). You might find this useful, miss. Hard. Hit him hard. (*He shakes his head.*) What shall he do with his money ! Feller that asks that doesn't deserve to have any.

(*He exits behind the bar.* JOAN *crosses to the door* L. *and opens it.*)

JOAN. Outside.

SAM. Eh ?

JOAN. You heard. Outside. And don't ask me if I'm coming with you. I'm not. Get weaving. Out.

SAM (*stubbornly*). I won't go.

(JOAN *crosses to the bar.*)

JOAN. We'll see about that. (*She picks up the mallet.*)

(TOM *enters behind the bar.*)

SAM. Hey ! Not that.

TOM. Hard. Hit him hard.

JOAN. Going, then ?

(SAM, *muttering, backs to the door* L.)

JOAN. And remember.
SAM. What ?
JOAN. No drinking.
TOM. That's right, ruin me.

(*He exits behind the bar.*)

SAM (*apostrophically*). Blimey ! Is it worth it ?
JOAN. You've got to make up your own mind about that.
SAM. Don't be daft. I'm just beginning to learn that when a feller falls he hasn't got a mind of his own.

(*He exits* L., *colliding with* HELEN *who enters at the same moment.* HELEN *carries her script.*)

HELEN (*looking after* SAM). The perfect gentleman. (*To* JOAN.) Doing well, aren't you ? Two on a string.

(JOAN *gives* HELEN *a long look.*)

JOAN. Got your eye on one of 'em, by any chance ?
HELEN. I'm sure I don't know what you're talking about.
JOAN. Save the shocked innocence for your acting. You're a big girl now, you know.
HELEN. And old enough not to want to continue such a childish conversation, I hope.
JOAN. All right, love, but if I were you I think I'd stick to art. Ta-ta for now.

(JOAN *crosses and exits* R. HELEN *frowns then, pacing to and fro, murmurs her lines.* RICHARD *enters* R. *and crosses to the tool-kit on the settle.* HELEN *sees him, and recites her lines louder to attract his attention.* RICHARD *rattles the tools.*)

RICHARD. Oh, I'm sorry.
HELEN (*pretending to be startled*). Oh, you gave me quite a start.
RICHARD. Didn't mean to make such a clatter. This (*he shows the pliers*) slipped.
HELEN. It doesn't matter.

(*They look at each other and smile.*)

HELEN. I'm so sorry about last night.
RICHARD. What ?
HELEN. The trouble at our house.
RICHARD. It was nothing.
HELEN. I was disgusted with Sam Balcombe.
RICHARD. I was just as bad.
HELEN. You're surely not classing yourself with *him*.
RICHARD. He gets excited too quickly, that's all. I forgot myself, I'm afraid.

HELEN. I thought his provocation beyond endurance. I'm sorry you had to have such an experience at our house. I'm sure it must have made you think us an awful family.

RICHARD. Oh, no, Miss Blair.

HELEN. You've no need to be so formal. My name's Helen. May I call you Richard ?

RICHARD. Why, of course—er—Helen.

HELEN. Have you—er—er—have you known our Joan long ?

RICHARD. Oh, no. We met at a dance.

HELEN. She's a fine girl.

RICHARD. Yes, she is, isn't she ?

(*There is a momentary embarrassed silence between them. They smile.*)

RICHARD. Well—er—I suppose . . . (*He backs slowly to the door* R.)

HELEN. This is a busman's holiday for you, isn't it ?

RICHARD. In a way—yes. I like doing it, though. It's a change from the Lancashire Electric.

HELEN. Is that where you work ?

RICHARD. Yes.

HELEN. Why, that's near us !

RICHARD. Is it really ? Where d'you work ?

HELEN. Marlowe's. General office.

RICHARD. Do you really ? I'll bet I've passed you many a time. Which bus d'you catch ?

HELEN. Oh, the twelve or the eighteen.

RICHARD. Then I *must* have passed you. I'll look out for you tomorrow night— that's if you don't mind.

HELEN. I'd love . . . Not at all.

RICHARD. Er. . . .

HELEN. Yes ?

RICHARD. Matter of fact I'll be using the bus myself for the next few days. Motor bike going in dock. You know. Spot of engine trouble.

(JAMES *enters* R. *and pulls in a property basket after him.*)

HELEN. I'll look out for you.

RICHARD (*taking a deep breath and beaming*). Fine. (*He turns to* JAMES.) How goes it, James ?

JAMES. Who *is* that feller ?

RICHARD. Which one ?

JAMES. Aubrey—whatever he calls himself. He's a pansy if ever I saw one. (*Quoting* BETTY.) "Tall, fair and good-looking"— in a pig's eye.

RICHARD. Why, what's he done to you ?

JAMES. Nothin'. An' what's more, he'd better not try, either.

HELEN. He's a highly intelligent and sensitive young man—*and* a good actor, into the bargain.

JAMES. The fairy king. I know. (*To* RICHARD.) What d'you make of this play. Screwy, isn't it ?

(RICHARD *winks at* HELEN.)

RICHARD. Ask Helen. She'll explain.

(*He exits* R.)

JAMES (*to* HELEN). Aye, and you'll have some more explainin' to do to our Joan if she cops you at this carry on, won't you, love ?

HELEN. I won't even deign to answer.

JAMES. Deign, eh. (*He whistles.*) This play's catching.

HELEN. Ignorance.

JAMES. Contempt, now ! Can't help it if it seems screwy to me, can I ? Look, I ask you. (*He takes a property donkey's head from the basket.*) A fellow's turned into a donkey and . . .

HELEN. Poetical imagination's wasted on you. It would be a perfect bit of casting if you took the part. But, if you don't mind I'll go where there's some sense.

(*She crosses and exits* R.)

JAMES. Me ! On the stage ! What a performance. (*Jealously.*) Aye, and that feller Aubrey. He ought to get his hair cut. Bet he's had it permed. Those waves aren't natural. Fancies his chances, that feller does. Well—but never mind. (*He looks at the donkey's head then glances around the room to see whether he is alone.*) Wonder what it feels ·like on ?

(*He dons the donkey's head, creeps to the bar and peers over it.* RICHARD *enters* R., *stops and stares.* MRS BLAIR *enters* L. *She carries a jug. She stands staring in surprise.* JAMES *makes a braying noise over the bar.* TOM, *looking startled, enters behind the bar, picks up the mallet and raps the donkey's head.*)

TOM. Gerrout of it.

JAMES (*quickly removing the head*). Hey, that was me. (*He rubs his head.*) What's the game.

MA. Why ! It's our James.

TOM. I thought it was a circus broke loose. Serves you right for acting the goat.

RICHARD (*laughing and applauding*). Full marks, James. You were good.

JAMES. He doesn't want to be so blooming handy with that mallet.

TOM. Aye ? And you should learn when to duck.

JAMES (*seeing* MRS BLAIR). An' what's brought you here, our Mother ?

MA. Well, you know how our dad likes a bit o' peace and quiet—an' as you were all out I thought I'd treat him to a drop of supper beer.

TOM. Nay. (*He turns and speaks off.*) Wonders'll never cease. What d'you think, Mrs Dorbell—I've got a customer.

JAMES. You've got another, too. Sit down, Mother, you're going to have one with me.

MA. No thanks, lad. I'd better be getting back to father.

JAMES. You can sit down for a minute. Dad'll be all right. Come on, now. No messin' about.

(JAMES *persuades* MRS BLAIR *to sit on the chair* L. *of the table* R. MRS DORBELL, *in a panic, enters* L.)

MRS DORBELL. Me purse! Me purse! (*She crosses to the settle.*) Ah! there it is. Nowt in it only pawn tickets, worse luck. (*She picks up the purse.*) Well, it's good to see you in here for a change, Mrs Blair.

MA. Hello, Nancy. No, our James, I really mustn't stay.

JAMES (*with finality*). You're having a drink.

MA. I'm not sitting here drinking alone.

MRS DORBELL. Well, I'm sorry I can't join you, love. I've had my ration for tonight, worse luck, an' even that was given me by Tom, God bless the lad.

JAMES. Give her another, Tom, an' a Guinness for Ma. (*To* MRS DORBELL.) And I know you weren't hinting. Oh, you haven't met Richard Sanders, have you Ma?

(TOM *draws a pint of beer and pours out a Guinness.*)

RICHARD. Good evening, Mrs Blair.

MA. Good evening.

JAMES. Got that shiner through our Joan.

RICHARD. I'm sorry about that, Mrs Blair. I didn't . . .

MRS DORBELL (*crossing and sitting* R. *of the table* R.). It was Sam Balcombe's fault. Trouble wherever he is.

(JAMES *planks the money down on the bar and takes the drinks to* MRS BLAIR *and* MRS DORBELL. RICHARD *crosses to* C.)

JAMES. There you are, Mother, love. An' all the best, Mrs Dorbell.

MA. Thank you, lad.

MRS DORBELL. Best of health, lad. Celebrating something?

MA. Yes, what's come over you, our James?

JAMES. I'm in the amateur dramatics, didn't you know?

MA. I don't know all the things you get up to.

RICHARD. Has she asked you?

JAMES. Who?

RICHARD. Our kid. About taking the part?

JAMES. What're you blathering about? What part?

RICHARD. The fellow who wears that. Bottom, the weaver.

JAMES. D'you mean . . . ? (*He holds out the donkey's head and looks incredulously at* RICHARD.) Can you see *me* wearin' *that*?

RICHARD } (*together*). We've just seen you.
TOM

JAMES. Aye, the one and only performance.

(MRS BLAIR *bursts into laughter*.)

MA. Our James on the stage ! What next ?

JAMES (*to* TOM *and* RICHARD). And as for seeing me with this on. That was just a bit of fun.

(BETTY *enters* R. JAMES *has his back to her*.)

RICHARD. It's all a bit of fun. I've got to take one of the parts. The bellows mender, that's me.

(MRS BLAIR *laughs*.)

MA. Our James on the stage ! That's the limit. I'm coming to see that.

JAMES. You're going to wait a long, long time, Ma.

BETTY. Somebody seems to have made their mind up.

JAMES (*turning to* BETTY). Before you ask me, Betty, the answer's no. Definitely no. (*He crosses to* L.)

BETTY (*to* MA). May I introduce myself, Mrs Blair ?

JAMES. Oh, I'm sorry. Miss Betty Sanders, Ma.

MA. Hello, love. (*She chuckles*.) Ay ! I'd give a lot to see our James on the stage. What a pantomime. (*She laughs*.)

JAMES. You've no need to think I couldn't do it if I wanted.

MRS DORBELL. Now we're getting warmer.

JAMES. But don't kid yourself, all the same. I'm not going to do it.

MA (*chuckling*). Can't get over it ! The very idea !

JAMES. Chuck it, Ma. It was bad enough being copped with this thing on my head.

TOM. Thought it was the real thing. Gave him a clout with this.

MRS DORBELL. Did it hurt you, love ?

JAMES. I can do without another like it.

BETTY. Try it on again and let me see.

JAMES. I'll do nothing of the kind.

MA. Oh, go on, our James. I haven't enjoyed myself so much in years.

MRS DORBELL. You wouldn't debar your Ma a bit of pleasure, would you ?

JAMES. I'm not putting it on.

MA. He used to be a proper mimic when he was a little lad. Mad half hour he used to have every night. And when it was full moon ! Well ! Laugh !

JAMES. Never mind the family secrets, Ma. I'm still not putting it on. I look daft enough without it.

BETTY. Are you fishing for compliments ?

JAMES. No. I'm just not going to be made look a fool.

BETTY. Have you thought you might be making me look a fool.

JAMES. How ?

BETTY. I'd a different opinion of you, that's all. If I'd have thought you were going to act like a self-conscious boy I'd never have suggested your name to the producer.

RICHARD. Cover up, James. Cover up. Watch those low punches.

(BETTY *tries to silence* RICHARD *with a look*.)

JAMES. Don't need to. I can take it. As for making you look a fool. If you'd asked me first . . .

BETTY. I didn't ask you first. I'm sorry.

RICHARD. Duck, James. Duck.

MA. Oh, go on, lad. Oblige the young lady.

(JAMES *shakes his head emphatically*.)

BETTY. There's no use my persisting ?

JAMES. No. Why don't you ask Aubrey ?

BETTY. He's already got a part.

JAMES. Which one ?

BETTY. The Fairy King.

JAMES. That ought to suit him. Thought he was a blooming girl with trousers on when I first saw him. Hair hanging half way down his back.

BETTY. Don't be personal.

MRS DORBELL. Sounds like he's getting jealous, to me.

JAMES. Jealous ? Me ? Of him ?

MA. What's this ? Our James interested in girls ?

JAMES. Who said I was ?

MA. Wait till dad hears about this. Wait till I tell him.

JAMES. Don't you go telling anything to anybody. (*To* BETTY.) When I make up my mind on a thing—take it from me, there's nothing more to be said. And understand *that*, Betty Sanders—if you know what I mean.

BETTY. And when it comes to people making up their minds— two can play at that game. And you understand *that*, James Blair.

(*She takes the donkey's head from* JAMES *and neatly pops it on his head*.)

If you know what I mean.

(*She exits* R.)

RICHARD. See what she means, James ?

JAMES, *entering into the spirit of the thing, brays and gives* RICHARD *a playful back kick as—*

the CURTAIN *falls*

ACT III

When the Curtain *rises,* Mr Blair *is seated in the armchair above the fireplace, reading a newspaper. He comes to the end of the article, shakes his head, sighs and tut-tuts.*

Pa. War in the offing again, eh ? And the last one hardly over. Aye, I dunno. (*He turns the page and resumes reading.*)

(*The sound of an animal-like roar is suddenly heard off upstairs.*)

(*He jumps and looks at the ceiling.*) My God ! Whatever was that ? (*He listens.*) What the dickens is our James up to now, I wonder.

(*The roar off is repeated.*)

(*He rises, muttering, crosses to the door up* R. *and calls.*) What's up with you, our James ? Are you all right ?
James (*off*). Of course I'm all right. Leave me alone.

(Mr Blair *returns to his chair, still muttering.*)

Pa. Never a dull moment in this blessed house.

(*As he flops into the chair there is a kick on the front door.*)

(*Irritably.*) Now who the hell's this ? (*He rises and goes to the door.*) No place like home, eh ? If it's those kids again I'll give 'em a belting. (*He opens the door.*)

(Mrs Dorbell *is revealed outside the door.*)

Oh, it's you, Nancy. Come in.
Mrs Dorbell (*entering*). Well, you don't think I'm going to stand out there on the step, do you ?
Pa. You usually walk in without knocking, if it comes to that. What's up now ?
Mrs Dorbell. Want some pennies for the gas. Can you change a thrip'ny bit ? That blooming meter's always on the beg.

(Mr Blair *searches his pockets for coins and exchanges* Mrs Dorbell's *threepenny piece for three pennies.*)

Where's everybody ?
Pa. Out, except our James. But what's come over him I don't know. (*He sits in the armchair above the fireplace.*)
Mrs Dorbell (*sitting* L. *of the table*). What's up with him ?

Pa. Don't ask me. He's got rid of 'em ; his pigeons. Wanted money urgently, he said.

Mrs Dorbell. I've been wanting it urgent all my life, lad.

Pa. Turned his blooming pigeon cote into a carpenter's shop. I must say he's made a nice dressing-table for a customer.

Mrs Dorbell. If those pigeons'd have been mine they'd have been in a pie long ago.

Pa. Don't be daft, Nancy. They were too expensive to eat.

Mrs Dorbell. Don't talk to me about eatin'. By gum ! When I think of it—when I was a child.

Pa. That was a long time ago, lass. And things have changed, Nancy.

Mrs Dorbell. Of course they've changed. There's that feller in the next street. Eleven kids. Thirteen of 'em with him and his wife in a two bedroomed house. Now they've given him a Corporation house and a fine mess that slut of a wife of his'll make of it.

Pa. Where does he work ?

Mrs Dorbell. Work ? *He* can't afford to work. Five pounds a week he draws with his family allowances for doin' nothin'—and the rent paid for him into the bargain.

Pa (*feelingly*). I'd want more'n five pounds a week to live in a house with eleven kids in it. Aye, even it if was rent free.

Mrs Dorbell. Don't worry, he's never in—except at bedtime. Gets his beer and cigarette money on the sly, runnin' for the bookie and openin' and closing motor car doors at the dog track. A feller that saves his money, buys his own house and doesn't have a tribe o' kids he can't afford—what do they do to him. Tax him. It's wrong, Jim Blair. It's wrong.

Pa. And it was wrong when three and a half million lads were left to rot on the dole. Look, Nancy, they're trying to give everybody a square deal—and there's bound to be some scroungers.

Mrs Dorbell. One crowd sayin' there's too many people in the country and t'other givin' 'em eight bob a week to have more.

Pa. That's one thing you'll never stop 'em from havin', anyway.

Mrs Dorbell. An' when they have 'em nowadays what do some of the young married uns want ? Somebody to sit in and look after 'em while they go out enjoyin' 'emselves.

Pa. That's a job for you, love.

Mrs Dorbell. I know it. But thank God I can pick my customers. Him and her with the eleven kids ! Puh ! I only sit in for gentlemen who understand.

Pa. What ?

Mrs Dorbell. My terms. Half a crown an hour, a quart o' Guinness and the radio.

Pa. By gum, you are in a mood tonight, Nancy.

(*The roar is repeated off.* Mrs Dorbell *jumps.*)

MRS DORBELL. What on earth's that ?

(MR BLAIR *rises in a fury and stamps to the door up* R.)

PA. This has gone far enough. (*He hammers on the stairs with his fist.*) What the devil's going on up there ?

JAMES (*off*). Oh, Pa, go away and leave me alone.

PA. I'll give you go away. Come you down this very minute.

JAMES (*off*). Aw ! Blooming heck.

(JAMES *stamps down the stairs and enters. He carries his script.*)

What's up with you ? I went upstairs out of everybody's way. Is there *anything* a fellow can do in this house without being disturbed ?

PA (*crossing and sitting in his armchair*). What the 'ell are you doing up there ?

MRS DORBELL. Thought it was a wild animal let loose in the house.

(JAMES *turns to* MRS DORBELL.)

JAMES (*immensely pleased*). Did you really ? Did you, Mrs Dorbell ? Did you really think I was a wild animal ?

MRS DORBELL. Never heard a more unearthly sound in all my life. Nearly jumped out of my skin.

JAMES. By gum ! Well, I'm pleased to hear that. (*He lights a cigarette and beams.*) What did you think it sounded like, Dad ?

PA. I'd just as soon be sitting in the zoo.

JAMES (*clicking his tongue*). I'll shake 'em.

PA. Shake who ?

JAMES. The audience. I've joined the amateur dramatics. I'm Bottom the Weaver and I'm changed into a donkey and the Fairy Queen makes love to me.

MRS DORBELL. He's going off his head.

PA. Are you all right, our James ?

JAMES. Course I'm all right. It's Shakespeare.

MRS DORBELL. I've never heard anything so daft in all my life.

PA. Why don't you take your amateur dramatics to the theatre where they belong ?

JAMES. We've got to learn our parts, haven't we ? What's more I was in my bedroom. What's more you're taking me out of the mood. Another thing, I'd like the house to myself for an hour, if you don't mind, Dad.

PA. You would, would you. And what for this time, might I ask ?

JAMES. Well, the young lady's coming round at any minute to rehearse with me. And don't ask me what young lady. It's the young woman who's playing the part of the Fairy Queen.

PA (*muttering*). Young women and fairy queens. I dunno.

JAMES. Nay, Dad, only to oblige. Thought you'd like to go to the pub for an hour.

PA. If that's the lark you've got on you can bet I'm not staying here.

MRS DORBELL (*settling herself*). Well, I'm not stirrin' a budge. I'm waiting here to see your Ma.

JAMES. You can't stay here, Mrs Dorbell. Not while I'm rehearsin'.

MRS DORBELL. I said I'm not shiftin' a hinch.

JAMES. Look here, Mrs Dorbell, you don't understand . . .

MRS DORBELL. *You're* the one that doesn't understand. I've got no money to go sitting in pubs.

JAMES (*taking some coins from his pocket*). There you are. Take it and hop it to the pub.

MRS DORBELL (*taking the coins*). Well, all right, then. But tell your Ma I'll be calling back later. (*She rises and crosses to the street door.*)

(MR BLAIR *puts his coat on, picks up his hat and follows* MRS DORBELL.)

PA (*muttering*). Fairy queens, now. What next? Come on, Nancy.

MRS DORBELL. Marriage. That'll be what's next. And don't forget it, James Blair. That bet's still on. Ten quid to a shirt button that you're off first.

(MR BLAIR *and* MRS DORBELL *exit by the street door.*)

JAMES. Married, eh? (*He closes his eyes and takes a deep, slow breath.*) What a wife! Me comin' home to her every night! Home o' my own, eh! (*He comes to earth.*) Better stop this and get down to studying. (*He glances at his part.*) Dunno how I'm going to learn all this. (*He paces down* R.)

(JOAN *enters by the street door.*)

(*He recites*). "Truly a peck of provender : I could munch your good dry oats. Methinks I have a great desire to a bottle of hay."

JOAN. Bottle of hay?

JAMES (*turning quickly*). Oh, it's you, is it? Well, before you start I don't want any interrupting. I'm studying.

(JOAN *turns to the chest of drawers, takes out a clean blouse and begins to change.* JAMES *affects absorption in his part.*)

JOAN. How's Sam Balcombe doing?

JAMES. Eh?

JOAN. Sam Balcombe. How's he doing? And I mean at work.

JAMES. You'd think he was on piece work the way he's carrying on. He's barmy, if you ask me.

JOAN. What's he been up too?

JAMES. Wanted me to go to night school with him. And why are you so interested in him, all of a sudden?

JOAN. It's my nature, don't you know ? How's your little affair going on ? And don't ask me who with.

JAMES. I don't know what you're talking about. (*He moves and sits above the table.*)

JOAN. Oho ! Did he fall or was he pushed. You've had it, chum. Setting up in business on his own. Why, you'll be washing your neck and changing your shirt next.

JAMES (*loftily*). I'm studying.

(HELEN *enters by the street door. She is dressed fashionably in a new outfit.* JOAN *stares at her.*)

JOAN. Who-ooooo ! The new look.

JAMES. Same old face, though. Who's the new bloke *this* time ?

HELEN. I should have thought you'd enough to do learning your part without interesting yourself in my business.

JAMES. Smells like monkey business to me.

HELEN. What are you insinuating ?

JAMES. If you two aren't double crossing each other I'll eat my hat.

JOAN. Why bring me in ?

JAMES. When are you packing it in with Richard ?

JOAN. *Am* I packing it in with him ?

JAMES. Why don't you play the white man, the pair of you ?

JOAN. What are you bleating about ?

JAMES (*pointing to* HELEN). You've got Sam Balcombe where you want him and she's giving Richard the come-on behind your back.

(JOAN *looks at* HELEN.)

HELEN. If I were it wouldn't be any business of anybody's. He's free, you know.

JAMES. I don't fancy his chances of keeping free much longer.

JOAN. Where that's concerned you've no room to talk, my bonnie lad-o.

(HELEN *looks from* JOAN *to* JAMES.)

Yes, take a good look at the dark horse. Where Betty Sanders is concerned he's swallowed the lot—hook, line and sinker.

(JAMES *grins.*)

And she'll soon wipe that grin off your face.

HELEN (*incredulously*). Betty Sanders going for you ?

JAMES. You've no need to look at me as though I was a displaced person. I *do* live here, you know.

JOAN. Mightn't be doing that much longer if I know anything about it. Got a house yet ?

JAMES (*tapping his forehead*). Might be using this for all you know. If her ladyship there gets away with the double cross and sees our Richard off there'll be room at the Sanders'. Aye, and they've got a garden there—and a bath.

(HELEN *turns away suddenly, crosses to the sideboard and stands with
her back to them.*)

See. Bull's eye.

JOAN. I can see.

(HELEN *turns on them abruptly.*)

HELEN. Oh, how can you be so insensitive ?

JOAN. Hullo, what have we got now ?

HELEN. There's no use kidding ourselves. We are thinking about
it—all of us. You know what I mean—marriage, that's what I'm
talking about.

JOAN. No need to go all dramatic. There's no law against it.

HELEN. Oh, can't you be serious for once ?

JAMES (*sympathetically*). What's biting you, love ?

(HELEN *struggles with her emotions for a second.*)

HELEN (*blurting it out*). It's us. All of us. Us, and Dad and
Mum. Even though we do have a row sometimes.

JOAN. Sometimes. Ohooo !

HELEN. All the time, then, if you'd rather have it that way. But
when I thought of us all then—getting married. Oh, I don't know.

JOAN. What the dickens *are* you getting at ?

HELEN. It's hard to explain. A strange feeling came over me
when I thought of us all leaving home. As though something was
coming to an end. It made me go all cold.

JOAN. Stand nearer the fire then.

HELEN. Oh—you . . .

JAMES (*thoughtfully*). I think I know what you mean, love. I
never thought of it like that before.

HELEN. Like what ?

JAMES. Like what you said. The old home breaking up. Aye,
and Ma and Pa being left on their own.

JOAN. Pa won't mind. He's looking forward to his peace and
quietness.

HELEN. You're the most aggravating . . .

JAMES. Here we go. There's one thing certain—if ever I do get
wed there'll be none of this argy-bargy in my house.

JOAN. That means you'll be the dumb man of Manchester, then.
But you get the house first.

JAMES. I'm not worried about that.

JOAN. You will be—when you try. You haven't a chance of one
till you've got half a dozen kids.

(JAMES *rises and crosses to the fireplace where, hands in pockets, he
raises himself on his toes and looks at the ceiling.*)

JAMES. Kids, eh ? (*He laughs.*) By gum !

JOAN. What's funny ?

JAMES. Just thinkin'. A little lad callin' me "Dad"! Aye, I go proper daft all over at the thought of it. (*He grins.*) Auntie Helen and Auntie Joan.

(HELEN *puts on an agonized expression.*)

HELEN. Oh!

JOAN. What's up with you now?

HELEN (*contemptuously*). *You'd* never know.

JOAN. I know—insensitive. That's me.

HELEN. Yes, as much imagination as a cow.

JOAN. Hey! Hey! Somebody's asking for it—new suit or no.

JAMES. Backyard, the pair of you, if you want to fight. Betty Sanders'll be here in a minute.

JOAN. She's used to scrapping in this house, what with the shiner Sam Balcombe gave to Richard.

HELEN. Sam Balcombe didn't get it all his own way.

JOAN. Oh, he didn't, didn't he?

HELEN. Richard half murdered him. And if any man deserved it Sam Balcombe did. The low bred spiv.

JOAN. Sam Balcombe's as good as Richard Sanders any day.

JAMES (*in mock despair*). Roll on me wedding day.

HELEN. You can have him.

JOAN. Don't talk about him as though he's something you give away with a pound of sugar.

HELEN. I'd be quite happy not to have to talk about him at all.

JAMES. Nice way to be towards your future brother-in-law.

HELEN. Will you —

JAMES
HELEN } (*together*). Mind your own business?

JAMES. Do you know where I'm going?

JOAN. You ought to know your way by now. You've been told to go there often enough.

JAMES (*crossing to the staircase door*). I'm going to my bedroom to study my part and when Betty comes I hope you'll have the decency to clear off and let's get on with the rehearsing. (*He pauses at the foot of the staircase.*) And in case you're thinking up a wisecrack about rehearsing I *mean* rehearsing.

(*He exits up the stairs.* JOAN, *humming to herself, picks up the comb from the mantelpiece, looks in the mirror and combs her hair.* HELEN *sits* R. *of the table, drums on it with her fingers tips and watches* JOAN.)

HELEN. You can be the most irritating creature.

JOAN. What's wrong with her majesty now?

HELEN. I want to know where we stand. I loathe hole and corner arrangements. What are you going to do about Richard Sanders?

JOAN. I don't know.

HELEN. You can at least say who you're in love with.

JOAN. Would it make any difference if I did ?

HELEN. Do you want to marry Richard ?

JOAN. It's manners to wait until you're asked. You ought to know that. You're the lady.

HELEN. Then he hasn't asked you ?

JOAN. Sometimes I think you're a bit tapped up here. One minute you're bleating to think of the old home being broken up and the next you can't break it up quick enough. If I were you I'd try making up my mind.

HELEN. I did. The first time he came here.

JOAN. And you'd only just ditched the other bloke. Not bad going, eh ?

HELEN. It's the truth, whether you like it or not.

JOAN. What makes you think he feels the same way about you ? Has he said so ?

HELEN. There's an understanding between you two isn't there ? How could he ?

JOAN. Oh, it's happened before, understanding or no.

HELEN. Richard's a gentleman.

JOAN. Oh, come off it. You've been ˙chinwagging with him about it, haven't you ?

HELEN. The situation has been discussed.

JOAN. That's right. Wrap it up—and don't forget the ribbon.

HELEN. You've no need to think there's been anything dishonourable.

JOAN. The honour stakes, now ! I'd like to have had a ringside seat at those.

HELEN. Must you reduce everything to vulgarity ?

JOAN. I'm made that way, didn't you know ? Besides, somebody's got to talk plain English.

HELEN. If you don't want to discuss the matter . . .

JOAN. What's to discuss ? As far as Richard's concerned it seems I've had it. So what ? I'm no breach-of-promise type.

HELEN. If you prefer to put it that way . . .

JOAN. I do. Though I'd have thought better of him if he'd told me himself.

HELEN. He will.

JOAN. Now isn't that nice of him ? I suppose if Sam Balcombe had done the ditching everybody'd have said it's all you could expect. Ah, well, Rcihard's a gentleman. The old, old story. Get a name for early rising and you can stay in bed all day.

(HELEN *regards* JOAN *thoughtfully*.)

HELEN. I've been awfully muddled about it all, Sis. You know, feeling all the time that I was playing a dirty trick. You don't think I did it on purpose ? You don't think I'd . . . ?

JOAN. Don't fret yourself about me, love. I shan't die wondering.

HELEN. I'm sorry for what I said about Sam, Sis. I didn't mean it.

JOAN. If we get wed he'll hear worse from me before he kicks the bucket.

HELEN. You are thinking of marrying him, then ?

JOAN. That depends on him.

HELEN. Oh, I wish I was like you.

JOAN. What have I done now ?

HELEN. You've always been the same. You ... Oh, nothing ever frightens you.

JOAN. What are you scared of ?

HELEN. I don't know. I—I ...

JOAN. Stop stammering.

HELEN. I can't put it into words. You're practical. I'm not. I—I ...

JOAN. "I—I ... " Chuck it and come down to earth.

HELEN. Don't tell me I'm acting.

JOAN. You're always acting. Face up to it. You're going to get married. You'll have two or three kids and lose your figure. Then— well, as far as I'm concerned I hope I turn out be as good as Ma.

HELEN. Oh, you make it all sound so cut and dried.

JOAN. And so it is. You kid yourself and I don't. You think Sam Balcombe's this and that.

HELEN. I've already apologized.

JOAN. You thought it, all the same, like everybody else does. If he'd been a dog with a lame paw you'd have gone all gooey over him. Well, he is a lame dog and I think I can put him on the beam again, aye, and do myself a bit of good, too. He's working now and I've stopped him spivving and boozing. But I'll see he has his pint when he wants it. He doesn't know it but he's mine. And I'm not saying he won't turn out bad when ... Oh well, I've seen other married men get fed up with their wives when there's a couple of kids around and there's some sacrificing to be done. If he turns out to be like some of the rest—(*she shrugs, then stares at* HELEN) I'll turf him out of my house and I shan't starve while I've got these. (*She shows both her hands.*)

HELEN (*thoughtfully*). It's that that really frightens me.

JOAN. What ?

HELEN. Getting old. The way things change.

JOAN. You're a fine one to talk about not wanting things to change. You've hardly put a new dress on without you're looking for patterns for another.

HELEN. Dresses ! You don't understand.

JOAN. No ? Trouble with you is you expect too much. All that boy-gets-girl-happy-ever-after stuff in those plays of yours. Not interested. Settle yourself to it. If you marry Richard you'll have a working lad's wage to make spin out and the first kid'll mean good-bye to that motor bike. That'll keep you busy, me old cockalorum.

And if you want to know, I'm looking forward to it, middle-aged spread and all.

(*There is a knock on the street door.* JOAN *goes to answer it.*)

This'll be our prospective sister-in-law. We'd better do a bunk and give the lad a chance. (*She opens the door to reveal* SAM BALCOMBE.) Oh, it's you.

(SAM *enters. He is spruced up, though still wearing working clothes.*)

SAM. Well, you've no need to make it sound as though I'm in the way.

(JAMES *enters down the stairs. He is beaming in anticipation of welcoming* BETTY.)

JAMES (*disappointed*). Oh, it's you.
SAM. That's what she just said. What's up with me, anyway ?
JAMES. Only one thing. You're breathing.

(*He exits and stamps up the stairs.* SAM *mutters something after* JAMES *then looks at* JOAN.)

SAM. Are you coming with me ?
JOAN. Where to ?
SAM. Well, I thought you'd like to walk as far as the night school. I'd pay for you to the pictures, then you could meet me coming out.
JOAN. Chucking your money about, aren't you ?
SAM. Aw, blimey, can't you understand ? (*He glances at* HELEN.) Never get a chance to talk to you except at weekend with night school every night. Besides, you've still not been to see the house.

(HELEN, *taking the hint, rises and moves* R.)

HELEN. Excuse me.

(*She exits down* R.)

SAM. What's up with her ? I've not said anythin', have I ?
JOAN. Oh, give over.
SAM. She never said good evening to me when I came in.
JOAN. Neither did I if it comes to that. (*She makes a sweeping bow.*) Good evening, Samuel. Feel any better now ?
SAM. Aw, Joan, why have we to go on like this ? You living here and me at our place. What's to stop us from . . .
JOAN. Save your breath, we've been over all this before.
SAM. Well, I don't see why . . .
JOAN. You don't have to. Just keep on as you're going.
SAM. But I've got . . .
JOAN. You haven't got me yet.
SAM. But time's going on.

JOAN. Then make the most of it. Pass those exams. The money you'll earn after that is the kind I want to see in your pocket. The other stuff's got wings.

SAM (*resigned*). I suppose you're right.

JOAN. Right or wrong that's the way it's going to be if it's me you want.

SAM. You I want! Do you think I'd do this for anybody else? (*Ingratiatingly.*) Come on, Joan. Walk with me to night school and let's have a look at that house. Just a look.

(*There is a knock on the street door.*)

JOAN (*moving to the street door*). All right. But I'm not going to make a habit of this. (*She opens the door to reveal* RICHARD *who stands on the step.*)

RICHARD. Oh, hullo.

(*He enters.* JAMES *enters hurriedly down the stairs.*)

JAMES (*disappointed*). Oh, isn't she coming? Your Betty?

RICHARD. I dunno. Were you expecting her?

JAMES. Course I am. We're rehearsing. And for the last five minutes I've done nothing but run up and down stairs.

RICHARD. Yes, and I ran out of petrol round the corner. Had to push my bike here.

SAM (*truculently*). Well, you can start pushin' it again if you think you're taking Joan out. She's coming with me.

JOAN (*warningly*). That'll do, there. That'll do.

(JAMES *stamps to the stairs.*)

JAMES. If *this* is starting, I'm off.

(*He exits up the stairs.*)

RICHARD. As a matter of fact, Joan, I'd like to have a word with you — alone.

SAM. In a pig's eye, you will.

RICHARD. I wasn't talking to you. And if it's trouble you want I don't mind taking up where we left off last time. But not here.

(SAM *is about to retort but* JOAN *anticipates him.*)

JOAN. You dare, that's all—and as far as I'm concerned you've had it.

(SAM *mutters.*)

And stop muttering, grumble guts.

(SAM *gives* RICHARD *a vicious look.*)

SAM. Let's get out of here, then.

(JOAN *crosses to the chest of drawers for her hat.*)

JOAN. Anything for a quiet life. (*To* RICHARD.) And as for seeing me alone—I know the answer already. Our Helen's told me.

RICHARD (*relieved*). And you don't think I'm ... ?

JOAN. What do you want me to do ? Sue you ?

RICHARD. I just felt—you know . . .

SAM. What is all this ? Puzzle corner ?

RICHARD (*beaming at* SAM). Nay, Sam. Matter of fact. . . .

JOAN. He's changed his mind. Our Helen's copped him.

RICHARD. Nay, Joan. Don't put it that way. As for us, Sam . . .

JOAN. Come on, come on. You'll both be falling on each other's necks in a minute. (*To* SAM.) School for you, my lad.

SAM (*with affected meekness*). Yes, Ma.

(JOAN *exits by the street door.* SAM *follows her and, as he passes* RICHARD, *he makes a circle of thumb and forefinger.* RICHARD *grins and holds up his thumb.* SAM *nods towards the door down* R., *then exits by the street door, leaving it open.* RICHARD *crosses quietly to the door down* R. *and calls.*)

RICHARD (*softly*). Yohooo.

(HELEN *enters down* R.)

They've gone.

(*They look at each other for a moment then embrace.*)

HELEN. Oh, Richard.

(BETTY *enters by the street door and stands just inside.*)

BETTY. Is this a rehearsal or the real thing ?

RICHARD (*grinning ; confused*). Oh, chuck it, our Bess. You'd better know it now or never. We're . . .

BETTY. Going to get married.

RICHARD. Who told you ?

BETTY. I'm a clairvoyant, master mind. Have you got a house ?

HELEN. We haven't looked yet. Think our Joan and Sam Balcombe have been lucky. He says he can get one.

RICHARD. It's about time somebody did something about it. Can't get a house if you haven't got a family, and if you get rooms and start having kids you're kicked out. Where do you start ?

BETTY. By saying "I will", then you hope for the best and trust the politicians.

RICHARD. The only thing I'd trust them to do is draw their wages. Come on, Helen, before the garage closes. (*He crosses to the street door.*)

(HELEN *crosses to the foot of the staircase.*)

HELEN. O.K. I'll call Hamlet down. (*She calls.*) James, the Fairy Queen's arrived. (*She follows* RICHARD *to the street door.*)

RICHARD. Cheerio, Sis,

HELEN. Be seeing you.

(HELEN *and* RICHARD *exit by the street door.* JAMES, *beaming, comes hurriedly down the stairs and enters. He stares at* BETTY, *moves slowly above the table, puts his script on it, then rubs the seams of his trousers with his palms.*)

BETTY. What are you looking at me like that for ?

JAMES. I'm—I'm just glad you've come, that's all.

BETTY. But you knew I was coming.

JAMES. I know. But when you're looking forward a lot to a thing, well—you turned up, anyway.

BETTY. Well, well, well. You are taking the job seriously. (*She indicates the script.*) How's the part ?

JAMES. That's all right. (*He rubs his chin and looks at her dubiously.*) It's t'other I'm worried about.

(BETTY *looks at* JAMES.)

You've need to look.

BETTY. Is there anything worrying you ?

JAMES. You've need to ask.

BETTY. I have asked. What is it ?

JAMES. It was Sam Balcombe started me thinking.

BETTY. What about ?

JAMES. This house.

BETTY. Why don't you come to the point ?

JAMES. It was the house he took me to see. Never stopped talking about it. Going to work and when we were coming home, aye, and when we were having us lunch.

BETTY. Our lunch.

JAMES. Eh ?

BETTY. It's "our lunch" not "us lunch".

JAMES. Pardon me. It's my education. Fourteen years in standard one.

BETTY. What is this about the house ?

JAMES. Aye, morning, noon and night he was on about it.

BETTY. Did he buy it ?

JAMES. I'll bet he wishes he could. 'Cause it's mine. I nipped in first and there's the receipt for the deposit. (*He gives a paper to* BETTY.) There's going to be blue murder when he finds out. Not that I'm worrying. It'll teach him to keep his big mouth shut.

BETTY. When are you moving ? (*She puts the receipt on the table.*)

JAMES. When I get wed.

BETTY. You—married ?

JAMES. Well, I've made a start in the right direction, haven't I ? I've got a house. And that's more than a lot of married 'uns can say.

BETTY. It's pretty fast moving for a woman hater, isn't it ?

JAMES. I'm not thinking of women. Where I'm concerned one'll do for me,

BETTY. If you were my husband I'd see to it that one would *have* to do for you.

JAMES. Would you ?

BETTY. I jolly well would.

JAMES. I'd like to see you try it on. By gum I would.

BETTY. James Blair, are you proposing to me ?

JAMES. Now we're getting somewhere. Betty Sanders, I am. I want you to be my leading lady for the rest of my natural. Come on, love, what do you say ?

(*He holds out his arms to her. She embraces him. They are about to kiss when the front door is flung open and* SAM, *enraged, makes a stormy entrance.*)

SAM. There you are, Jim Blair.

JAMES. Aye, here I am and it's manners to knock. What's the matter with you ?

SAM. He stands there as cool as a cucumber with what he's got on his conscience and he asks me . . .

JAMES. There's nothing on my conscience.

SAM. Then you musn't have one. You dirty, double crossing . . .

JAMES. Here, here. That'll do.

(MR BLAIR *and* MRS DORBELL *enter by the street door and stand just inside it.*)

SAM. Of all the stinking, low down tricks. But you're not going to get away with it, James Blair. You're not going to get away with it.

JAMES (*indicating the receipt*). See that ? It's a receipt for the deposit—and it serves you right.

SAM (*spluttering*). Serves me right. Hear him ! Serves me right. An' he was the one who said he'd help me. Wanted to see a lad happy.

JAMES. Well, I'm the lad. And I'm happy. What's more, if I take anybody into partnership I want somebody who knows when to keep his big mouth shut. Let this be a lesson to you—or no partnership.

SAM. Come outside and I'll shut yours for you now.

PA. *Now* what's going on in here ?

MRS DORBELL. It doesn't sound as though they're going to play ring-o-roses.

SAM. I'll ring-o-roses him. Come on, Jim Blair, before your Joan gets back and stops me.

PA. Remember whose house this is, Sam Balcombe.

JAMES (*to* SAM). You know what you want, don't you ? You want a house.

PA. What the devil *is* all this about a house ?

SAM. The one I was going to get. My house it was and he snaked in behind my back and got it.

PA. What blooming house ?

JAMES. The one we're going to live in. (*He beams.*) It gives me great pleasure to present the future Mrs Blair, Pa. (*He hands* BETTY *to* MR BLAIR.) There you are Pa. Kiss your future daughter-in-law.

PA. Well, well. I never.

MRS DORBELL. This is very interesting. When are you getting wed ?

JAMES. Soon as we can. The house is there and I'm ready to-morrow.

MRS DORBELL (*holding out her hand*). In that case I'll collect now, James Blair.

JAMES. What ?

MRS DORBELL. Ten quid. Ten quid to a shirt button. That was the bet that you'd get wed first. Come on. Pay up.

BETTY. Nobody gets paid till the horse is past the post.

JAMES (*expansively*). Come on, all of you. Off to the pub and I'll buy you all a drink to celebrate. As for you, Sam, when you get wed I'll get my missis to let you have a couple of rooms.

BETTY. Two women in one kitchen ? Not likely.

SAM. I wouldn't share the blinking house with you. And you know what you can do with your drink ?

JAMES. Aye, sup it. Never mind, Sam, when we go into partnership the first job we'll do is to build you a house—when they take the controls off.

SAM. By the time they're off I'll have whiskers down to my knees. But don't you worry, James Blair. I'll have my own back.

(*He exits by the street door.*)

JAMES. Come on, all of you.

MRS DORBELL. This is going to cost you a packet.

BETTY. I wouldn't bank on that, Mrs Dorbell.

JAMES. Come on, Dad lad.

PA (*moving to the fireplace*). It's my feet, lad. I'll wait for your Ma. She'll be home in a minute. We shan't be long.

JAMES. O.K. Come on, Betty love. Come on, Nancy.

(BETTY *and* JAMES *move to the street door.*)

Ay, by gum ! I feel as though I could fly.

MRS DORBELL. Fly, eh ? When there's any free drink knocking around I'm jet propelled.

CURTAIN

FURNITURE AND PROPERTY LIST.

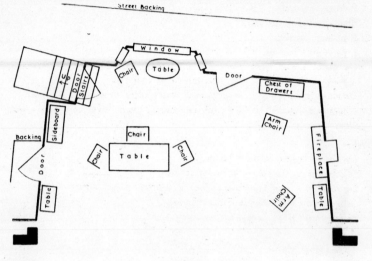

ACT I

On stage—

Kitchen range.

2 armchairs. *On them :* cushions.

Chest of drawers. *On it :* vases, papers, Mrs Blair's hat, other dressing as required.

> *In drawers :* clean blouse, clean socks, frock paper pattern, scissors, box of pins.

Oval table. *On it :* vases, letters, framed photographs, other dressing as required.

Occasional table (*down* L.). *On it :* play script.

Small table (*down* R.). *On it :* runner, radio receiver, copy of the "Radio Times", ornaments as dressing.

Sideboard. *On it :* runner, vases, handbag, other dressing as required.

> *In drawers :* carpentry design book.

> *Under it :* pile of magazines, and periodicals.

Dining-table. *On it :* white cloth, places laid for four, 3 used, 1 clean at left end, salt, pepper, basin with sugar, jug with milk, pot with tea, cups, saucers, plates, knives, forks.

4 dining chairs.

Carpet on floor.

Carpet on stairs.

Hearth rug.

Fender.

Fire-irons.

Pictures on walls.

Shaded electric pendant.

1 pr net curtains.

1 pr draw curtains.

On hooks behind front door : coat hangers, Mrs Blair's coat. *In coat pocket :* 5 ration books. Various other coats, etc.

On mantelpiece : clock, scissors, comb, vases, other dressing as required.

Under mantelpiece : string for drying smalls. *On it :* oven cloth, tea-towel.

Over mantelpiece : mirror.

Set—

On range : kettle of warm water.

In oven : meal for Helen on covered plate.

On table at R. *end :* newspaper, pencil, football pools coupons.

In armchair above fireplace : newspaper.

In armchair below fireplace : novelette.

Off stage—

Tray (MRS BLAIR).

Earthenware bread-mug. *In it :* bread (JAMES).

Soap, towel (JAMES).

Enamel mug. *In it :* cold water (JAMES).

Personal—

JAMES : cigarettes, matches.

SAM : flashy case with cigarettes, lighter.

MRS BLAIR : purse.

ACT II

SCENE I

Strike—

Everything from table R.C., newspapers, towel, soap, Pa's boots and socks, enamel mug.

Set—

On string under mantelpiece : James' collar and tie. Chair L. of table to face fire.

Clock to read 6.20.

Off stage—

Parcel. *In it :* length of dress material (HELEN). Drawing board (JAMES).

Personal—

JOAN : hand mirror, lipstick.

RICHARD : packet of cigarettes, matches.

SCENE 2

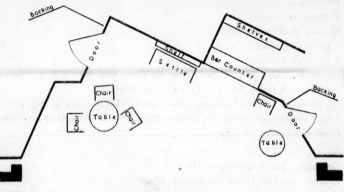

On stage—
 Settle. *On it :* roll tool-kit with a pair of pliers and other tools.
 Table L. *On it :* ashtray, mats.
 Table R. *On it :* ashtray, mats.
 4 chairs.
 Mirror over settle.
 Carpet.
 Spittoon.
 Advertisements on walls.
 On bar shelves : bottles of beer, spirits and minerals, optic measures and other dressing as required.
 Under bar counter : 2 bottles of ginger beer, 2 pints beer, glass of Guinness, mallet, tea-towel, dish-cloth, bottle opener.

Set—
 On bar counter : newspaper.

Off stage—
 "Temple Shakespeare" (BETTY).
 Screwdriver (RICHARD).
 Script (HELEN).
 Property basket. *In it :* donkey's head (JAMES).
 Jug (MRS BLAIR).

Personal—
 MRS DORBELL : duster, purse.
 JAMES : handkerchief, coins.
 SAM : coins.

ACT III

Setting as Act I.

Set—
 On armchair above fireplace : newspaper.

Personal—
 MRS DORBELL : 3d piece.
 MR BLAIR : 3 pennies.
 JAMES : cigarettes, matches, coins, script, receipt.